Praise for

Body of Time, Soul of Eternity

"Jerry Thomas has clarified ageless mystical wisdom in a way that makes it authentic and accessible to all souls searching for God Communion. I would particularly recommend it to clergy and spiritual directors regardless of denomination or faith tradition." — *The Reverend Susan Creighton, Episcopal Priest*

"*Body of Time, Soul of Eternity* brilliantly blends the fundamental truths of both the Western and Eastern mystical traditions. It is clear, concise and inspirational for all souls who are looking to know God and find true meaning in their life." —*Mukund Raj, Founder and Chairperson of the Shirdi Sai Baba Foundation of America*

"The message is simple. Only through the Heart can we find our way back Home—back to the Source, back to God. So how do we get there? *Body of Time, Soul of Eternity* provides an illuminated scaffolding where Eastern and Western mystical teachings merge to show us how to go within and find our way back Home." — *Jacqueline Sweeney, author of Kids Express*

"... *Body of Time, Soul of Eternity* provides the map and vehicle for the journey into the loving heart of God, our Essence....When I am alone and quiet, whether I scan through or contemplate a single passage, I always have a personal retreat experience of joy and silence within." —*Judy Gurley, author of Alters, A Simple Path to Emotional Wellness*

"Jerry Thomas, beloved spiritual brother to many and teacher/ philosopher to thousands, is a storyteller in the truest sense. In this book he weaves the Truth spoken by the ancient and immortal Ones and lulls us back to the only place of knowing the Being of God...in the Inner Silence of our Heart." —*Deeanne Bevin, healer, teacher, and long-time practitioner of Mystical Spirituality*

Body of Time
Soul of Eternity

Mystical Spirituality

Body of Time
Soul of Eternity

Mystical Spirituality

Jerry Thomas

Body of Time, Soul of Eternity: Mystical Spirituality

ISBN 1-59457-992-X

Library of Congress Control Number: 2004113734

Printed in the United States of America

Dedication

This book is dedicated to the great spiritual truth:

"Seek first the Kingdom of Heaven,
and all else shall be added unto you."
(Luke 12:31)

Note to Readers

This book is a condensed guide to the principles and understanding of Mystical Spirituality—the quest for the direct experience of God, the Ultimate Reality.

I open with the acknowledgement that finite words cannot bear the burden of describing the infinite any more than the mind can understand that which transcends it. Mysticism is the experience of the Source and Essence beyond its manifestations of form and thought. This material cannot be learned by the intellect. It is "remembered" in the heart of the Soul. It awakens a deep spiritual understanding which comes from our true nature.

The ideal way to read this book is to go slowly and to stop frequently to contemplate the Truths gathered from the God-Realized Beings, the mystics, who lived and expounded them over the centuries.

Some passages read like text and, from time to time, certain sentences are in bold type or put in a different font to emphasize something that captures the essence of a topic.

Most of what you read will not sound new at all. What we have done is synthesize very deep and meaningful understandings for a modern-day audience, and structured the sequence so that each section builds on the previous one.

The primary focus is the three questions that all nescient beings continuously ponder as life flows through them: Who am I? Where am I going? How will I get there?

This book sets out to answer these questions as the Great Masters of past and present have described the great adventure of life—the return Home to our One Source.

With Love and Great Peace along your journey,

Jerry Thomas
Derry, New Hampshire
November, 2002

Contents

Introduction

Perspective

Nothing short of the direct experience of God
will ever satisfy our needs for
wholeness, fulfillment and completion

Body of Time, Soul of Eternity is about the ageless Mystical Path of Union with God. It is not a path of the Old Age, nor is it of the New Age: it is beyond age, beyond the limitations of time. It is the Way of the Mystic.

Mysticism is living beyond the dream of duality

Over the years many of us have left traditional religion, searching for something that is bigger than we are, something that gives meaning and fulfillment in a world of continuous change and disappointment. The great saints and philosophers of both East and West have repeatedly told us that what we are looking for is hidden deep within us. It is the "pearl of great price," or "the Kingdom of Heaven which is within."

The Absolute Unchanging is the basis of relativity and change. Silence is the basis of activity. The merging of our inner nature as Silence and our outer nature as activity provides the full value of life. It is the union of the Kingdom of Heaven within and without. Mystical Spirituality is the marriage of all forms with their Divine Source, and the ensuing life is far from that of the remote contemplative. Rather, it is that of the inspired instrument of the Divine Will within creation.

The merging of our inner nature as Silence
and our outer nature as activity
provides the full value of life

God-Realized Beings, those who have achieved and embody the full value of the Creator within creation, and the God beyond the illusory play of duality, have boldly declared that man's essential nature is transcendent: it is the capacity for the complete realization of God while in human form. They see that Creation is God's Play. It is a play in which Essence takes form. The One becomes the many. Then the many differentiate, each becoming unique as they experience the One's myriad forms. Finally, each individual essence begins the mystical process of returning to its Source, knowing and merging with its True Self once again. In mystical spirituality, the process of life is the journey home while living fully in this world of created forms.

Essence takes Form
Form differentiates
then returns to Essence

The desire of Eternal Oneness to enjoy Its nature in many different forms is the impetus of the drama of the universal cosmic dream. Hence, creation is the act of repulsion from Source, a descent to matter. Spiritual Evolution is, in fact, the reversal of the creation process—the ascent to Source.

Man is the capacity for God

Empirical, rational and contemplative (direct) experience show us that all forms, from subatomic particles and elements of nature to star systems and the universe itself, are programmed to follow sequentially three primary commands: (1) go forth and experience, (2) become all you can be, and (3) come back Home. The Mystical Path of Coming Home is spirituality that transcends age, dogma, religion, culture, and personal ego. It outlines the journey of the human being through four primary states of realization.

> *Consciousness of Being; Soul Consciousness; The Soul aware of its own nature.* This first realization is that of the permanent fulfillment and bliss of the Soul, which replaces the transitory pleasures and pains of the limited ego self. It is about moving the point of identification from "I am the body, mind, and senses" (ego consciousness) to "I am the Inner Self" whose nature is ineffable Wisdom, Joy, Peace, and Love. This is moving from ego consciousness to Soul Consciousness. It is sometimes referred to as enlightenment: "The Kingdom of Heaven within."

> *Consciousness of the Source of Being; God Consciousness.* After attaining identity with Soul, the Soul realizes its unity with its Source which is God as the Creator. This is moving to awareness of the Source of the individual Soul and to the exquisite relationship in which the Soul knows its Divine Beloved and communes with It as the source of its very self.

> *Unity Consciousness; Christ Consciousness; Creation and Creator are One.* This is the state of awareness of God as the source of the individual self and God the source of all forms of creation. It is merging into God within

all of Its creation. As the Soul becomes more aware, it finds itself one with All That Is. This is the unity with God within creation. For the individual's experience, the universe is his body and all things that happen in the universe are his sensations.

Cosmic Consciousness. Ultimately, the Soul experiences the realization of Mystical Union with God beyond creation. "I and the Father are One." This is living as the mystic who is beyond the dream of reality. Truly "in the world, but not of it."

This spirituality transcends the ego's desire
to create personal reality
and fulfills the Soul's destiny to know
and become one with Ultimate Reality

Until we reach beyond the ego state (the state of separation), and fully attain the experience of the Soul as our state of being (the State of Grace), we are overshadowed by the experiences of everyday life. We experience suffering, which is the natural consequence of the separation from God and our

Inner Self. We lose our sense of security, purpose and connection to the greater whole. We are living outside of Wholeness and Unity as a separate entity, out of harmony with our Inner Self, out of balance, experiencing the polarity of excitation without the ground of Silence to support it. We are bound by the karmic laws and consequences of thoughts, deeds, and feelings that are alien to this Oneness. Pain on this earth plane is part of having a body and all that goes with the extreme paradox of being pure Spirit locked in a small human form with needs, desires, and cravings which the body inherited from its primitive physical and psychological nature. But suffering does not have to be part of our earth experience. The alleviation of suffering and the bliss of Union with God is the goal of Mystical Spirituality. There is an old Sufi saying that says it so well:

"The human being returning to God
is the pinnacle of Creation."[1]

The path to our inner nature is a simple one—so simple that it is overlooked in our rush to fill our lives with more and more of that which will never fulfill us. It is a subtle shift in focus and an expansion of perspective. The path is allowing for Silence and silencing the inner noise that hides the higher states of evolution and consciousness. It is a reversal of the life energy. It is a turning of focus from out to in, from excitation in the world of change to the profound peace resident in the inner state of Silence. It is a gradual inner progression from the State of Grace in Soul Consciousness with its inherent states of Love, Peace, Wisdom, and Joy, to the ecstasy of Divine Communion.

Mystical Spirituality reveals that these states are our inner nature. They exist within us already. They are not external possessions to be struggled for, but subtle awareness to be "allowed" and realized. Mystical Spirituality is the path of the Divine Feminine. It is a path of Silence and Grace.

The goal of Mystical Spirituality is a profound experience, an experience that:

Replaces the desperate need to control
with the sweetness of Surrender

Satisfies the mind's desire
for absolute understanding
with the Soul's longing for Faith

And, above all, replaces the state of emptiness
with the State of Grace

Mysticism is the path of the direct experience of the four spiritual realizations of God, our Essence:

> God as our inner self (individual aspect of God)
> God as Creator (Mother aspect of God)
> God within creation (the aspect of Christ Consciousness or the Son)
> God beyond creation itself (the Absolute Father aspect)

The Mystical Path is "The Path of Coming Home" to who we truly are. It is retracing the steps back to Source.

The universal goal of human life is to attain abiding happiness (bliss) in the midst of the fleeting series of pleasures and pains, which characterize life on this material plane, this plane of duality. This bliss can be found only in realizing the nature of the Soul, which is God within.

Bliss itself is the essence of the Divine. Attaining bliss marks the cessation of all suffering. It provides an unshakable state of inner equanimity, fulfillment, love, and joy without bounds. It is the state of the Inner Self. It is not subject to change. It is not overshadowed by external events, nor can it be affected by the body, mind, and senses. It is ever changeless, yet an ever-new Joy. This state of bliss is our natural state; it is what has been referred to as the "Kingdom of Heaven Within." It is the state of spiritual evolution in which we are fully united with the Essence of Divinity that is within—the Soul.

"We shall not cease from exploration

And at the end of all our exploring

Will be to arrive where we started

And know the place for the first time." [2]

Mystical Spirituality

The ancient Greek philosophers maintained that a life worth living is in direct relation to the quality of the questions we ask and the nature of the answers we accept. Mystical Spirituality addresses the three primary inquiries of human existence:

Who am I?

Where am I going?

How do I get there?

To know **"Who Am I?"** we explore creation and its five elements:

- the nature of Source (or God)
- the nature of man
- the purpose of creation
- the nature of this existence (duality)
- the highest meaning and purpose of our life

To know **"Where Am I Going?"** we first explore the seven states of consciousness that mark the journey of the Soul. We will also explore the five dominant paradigms from which we view our journey. These paradigms are reflections of what we believe to be the highest goals we can achieve. They also state clearly what we believe to be the purpose of our lives.

And to know **"How Do I Get There?"** we explore Mystical Spirituality, the spiritual path that brings us to Union with God —the Path of Coming Home. This is not a path of philosophers, teachers, or even the illumined ones. It is the path of those whose nature is one with God; those who not only know "I Am" but have become the "I Am." These are the God-Realized Ones...the true mystics whose forms are a pure reflection of Absolute Essence.

What makes us seek the Truth (the Changeless)? Although the process is driven by the yearning of the heart, we continuously and unsuccessfully attempt to use the mind to fulfill it. We seek the ocean, yet settle for a nautical map. We mistake knowledge about Truth with Truth itself. The problem with knowledge is that God (Truth) transcends the human intellect; it simply cannot be contained by human concepts. Knowledge of theology cannot provide the "I know." Knowledge is like a "menu," and it can never substitute for the experience of "I am," which is the "meal." Reading and understanding about the Wisdom, Peace, Joy, and Love of Inner Divinity cannot make these states spontaneously happen. The mind can attempt to put together fragments to make a picture of what a whole could look like, but Truth *is* the Whole, not an image. And it is the heart that knows, loves, and cherishes the Wholeness. Truth is known from the heart of one's being, the core, the "nous."

The mind can know the diversity of creation and forms, but only the Soul can know Unity and God.

We often settle for the menu and miss the meal!

Chapter One

Who Am I?

God

God is pure Essence.

The answer to the first inquiry, "who am I?" starts with forming a workable idea about the Source of all, the Prime Cause— God. The idea that the infinite, unlimited God could ever be defined or understood by the finite, limited human mind is a challenge that cannot be overcome. However, some idea of God in Mystical Spirituality, no matter how seemingly inadequate, is necessary to have a point of reference, which later is transcended and made ecstatically whole beyond all possible anticipation.

So many philosophies dismiss the value of any conception of God since ultimately all concepts do not fit. However, when we are crossing a river we need a boat. When we are on the other side it may be appropriate to discard the boat, but not before we even start our journey, and certainly not in the middle of the river. Concepts of God are also like wooden planks in a staircase. When you get to the destination, you no longer need them, but don't refuse to use a staircase to go up just because it ultimately doesn't serve you once you have arrived!

God is that which contains all that is, that which is the potential for all that could ever be or ever has been, and that beyond which no greater can possibly be conceived. God is Absolute, Unbounded, Omniscient, Omnipotent, and Omnipresent. Its nature is pure Existence (Being), pure Consciousness (Intelligence), and pure Bliss (which is characterized by the inner states of Peace, Joy, Love, and Wisdom). However, God manifests Its various aspects in the different states of higher consciousness: as an individualized being in the Soul; as creator in pure God Consciousness; as the consciousness that is within and supporting of all creation in Unity or Christ Consciousness; and in Cosmic Consciousness as the Essence of All That Is, the Absolute, Unmanifest Being beyond creation.

Man

Man is the capacity for God.

Man is an intelligent manifestation of creation, animated by Soul and overshadowed by a mistaken sense of identity with a body, mind, and senses (the ego). We are deluded into searching for happiness in an external world, forgetting that what we truly seek is the Divine bliss within. We are essence or spirit locked into an animal form with all of the limitations and ensuing needs for food, safety, security, pleasure, and control that are inherent in having a body. This misidentification with the body and inherent sense of separation is known as "ignorance."

Knowing that we are the "I Am" is enlightenment

Union with the "I Am" is our destiny—

God Realization

Who are we when we are in ignorance (ego consciousness)? We are the sum total of our desires, cravings, hopes, and fears. We are the effect these have on our selves, others, and our environment. We look outward for what is ours within. We live in incompleteness.

Who are we in enlightenment (Soul Consciousness)? When in enlightenment, we are free from the suffering that comes from not knowing the True Self and living in ignorance. We become the witness and live a life that is not overshadowed by external conditions.

Who are we in the God-Realized state (various states of God Realization)? We are perfect instruments of the Divine Plan, and our very presence within creation is an act of love and transformation for all entities and all realms. **We are complete —"perfect as the Father in heaven is perfect."** [3]

The Story of Creation

All relationships are founded on the basis of affinity, communication, and a common sense of purpose and understanding or "ground of being." An understanding of another's view of the purpose of creation is a profound indicator of his relationship with God, his perspectives, philosophy, identity, state of consciousness, beliefs, attitudes, and overall experience of life. An understanding of another's idea of the purpose of creation provides a view of his highest potential for spiritual growth.

The great Twentieth century mystic and God-realized Master, Paramahansa Yogananda, said that:

> The desire of Spirit to enjoy Its singular nature in many forms spawns the drama of the universal cosmic dream. The Master Dramatist has manifested throughout that cosmos an inconceivable ingenuity and inexhaustible variety. To unrealities He has given seeming reality. And yet, why must the show go on? It is God's lila (sport). He has a right to separate Himself into many if He so chooses. The point of it all is for man to see through His trick. If God did not cover Himself with the veils of maya (or delusion), there could be no cosmic game of creation. We are permitted to play hide-and-seek with Him, and try to find Him and win the grand prize. [4]

There is another more entertaining story along the same basic idea that I like to tell at retreats for those who are not well versed in mystical perspectives:

> So, here we have God, sitting somewhere in heaven contemplating His existence and thinking: 'Here I am, perfect in all ways. I am unbounded, absolute, all knowing, all-powerful, all loving—yet somehow I am incomplete! I have never known limitation. I have never differentiated my pure being. I am like this magnificent, unblemished crystal—perfect, and boring!
>
> I think that I will manifest Myself in form as a myriad of universes and experience all facets of My creation. I will send out from My Very Being individual aspects of Myself (Souls) to know this creation. But there is a problem here! If they go out and know that they are an individualized aspect of Me in creation, they will never know limitation; they will never differentiate. So what I will do is make them forget their Divine Nature. They will forget that they are Me and think that they are "them." I will command them to go forth; to experience and be all that they can be; and then I will call them home to Me. I will be complete having known incompleteness. I will be differentiated knowing separateness; and My One Identity

will be full and complete by including their identities as a part of Me.

God has five responsibilities in this great sport of creation: that of creating, maintaining, destroying, concealing (His true nature), and revealing (it is He who must ultimately reveal Himself to us).

So, we are innocently playing our role in the great drama of the cosmic dream. Even being lost in duality is part of our journey.

Creation

The One becomes many

The many differentiate

and return to the One

(The rest is commentary!)

Creation is an act of repulsion from the source—a descent of Spirit into matter.

Spiritual evolution reverses the creation process, the transcending of matter and a returning to the Source.

Creation is movement and modulation of the Infinite Silence. It is the Unbounded dreaming boundaries. It is perfect Wisdom experiencing ignorance of its true nature. It is Pure Bliss experiencing pain, happiness, and suffering. It is the unity of the Whole, of Love Eternal, living the illusion of loneliness and fear. What a paradox it is that the Supreme Absolute desires to experience Its absolute nature within the confines of Its relative manifestation, that God is dreaming us as these little mind, body, and sense egos.

God is Essence—Silence
Creation is form—
vibration on the surface of Silence

Ultimately there is only One, but there appears to be many, just as there is only one ocean with many waves. The waves are not the ocean. They are limited and cannot contain the vast ocean, but the ocean can contain the waves. The apple cannot contain the form, the vastness or wholeness of the tree, but the tree contains the apple. It is similar to understanding that "I am not the body, nor is the body me." The body is an aspect of my self, one very limited, temporary, and finite expression. And so, creation is a reflection of its Creator, limited by time, space, and finite existence; it cannot contain the fullness of the Nature of its Source. A two-dimensional image in a mirror cannot adequately reflect Infinite Dimension.

Limited form cannot contain Unbounded Essence
but Unbounded Essence can contain limited form

The "structure" of the cosmic dream is the modulation of Silence. It is "Spirit," the Creator, "breathing" waves of form onto the unbounded ocean of formlessness.

What perpetuates the "reality" of the dream is ignorance of the One. It is experiencing individual life as separate and outside the union with Oneness.

The dream is experienced so realistically because of mental excitation, which is a habitual focusing of the life energy and attention without. Waking from the dream is achieved by discovering and experiencing the essence of who you are while in the activity. Waking from the dream is seeing through this illusion and experiencing that there is only One.

Enlightened ones know that there is only One

God-Realized Beings are one with that Oneness

Duality

Duality is the nature of creation.

When Unity manifests as "the many," all forms are under the influence of the opposing opposites, or duality. Black and white. On and off. Life and death. Poverty and wealth. Sickness and health. All things are subject to inevitable transformation and change. This includes not only the physical planes of the grosser mind, body and senses, but the more subtle planes, the paranormal and the metaphysical realms of existence such as energy, vibration, and light. Today, metaphysicians describe man as having three bodies that cover the essence of the Soul: a physical body, an astral body, and an etheric (light) body. However, if it is of creation (subject to change), it is not who we truly are, no matter how seemingly subtle and sublime. Sound, vibration, and light are not our First or Ultimate Source. They are still manifestations. They are our temporary forms, not our infinite essence. We have *Bodies of Time, but Souls of Eternity.*

The experience of reality (duality) is the ever-changing play of opposites.

Ultimate Reality is changeless and its threefold nature—Existence, Consciousness, and Bliss immeasurable—is beyond time, space, and the limitations of the created realms.

Relativity (even the most subtle realms, as indicated previously) is characterized by a complex sequence of continuous alternation between the extremes of common opposites: the alternation of pleasure and pain; life and death; sickness and health; old age and youth. And as night alternates with day, fame with obscurity, poverty with fortune, war with peace, all forms come and go. Relativity is the play of light and energy subject to the direction and matrices of intelligence. The Source of the Intelligence that precedes energy and all subtle elements of creation is beyond duality.

Energy is a subtle form
of the substance of duality—
it is not the fabric of Ultimate Reality

Essence remains changeless. Forms are continuously in a state of flux. One of the greatest teachers in the relative world is death. Inevitably, one day all that we have ever worked for, all that we have believed and thought, and all we have loved so dearly will be taken away in the unavoidable transition of death. However, it is the nature of the delusion that we crave stability and peace where we know it's not—in the world of change and tumultuousness that we try so desperately to arrange as we like it to be, a world of "personal reality" that is given meaning by what we have, feel, experience, and achieve.

Absolute control of our personal reality is as futile as the effort of a little child by the seashore who tries to make the unrelenting ebb and flow of the ocean's mighty tides come to a permanent standstill...at a comfortable spot...on the shore...near his fragile little castle of sand.

The "relative" is characterized by a virtual infinite variety of polarities: positive and negative, male and female, yin and yang, light and dark, good and evil. The only constant in duality is change. Our greatest delusion is that we can control it.

Our primary fear is the fear of loss—
loss of objects, feelings, people, relationships
and all those things that we can never fully possess

Our primary grief is for the loss of
that which seeks to possess us (God)

Our primary illusion is in settling for the toys
instead of the Divine Toy Maker

Soul

The Soul, the Inner Self, is God dwelling within.

The Soul is the individualized aspect of the Divine Itself whose nature is Existence, Consciousness, and Bliss unbounded.

> The Soul is the purest sense of the individualized Being knowing its true identity as an aspect of God, living in the State of Grace, which is Love, Peace, Wisdom, and Joy while using the instruments of body, mind, and senses as a means to communicate and interact with objectified creation.

When the individual lives from the point of reference of the Inner Self or Soul, then he is in harmony with the laws of nature and the individual will becomes an instrument of the Divine Will. Right action and the fruits of the Spirit (Love, Peace, Wisdom, and Joy) become his state of being and flow effortlessly. All responses to life are evolutionary and bring all of life to a higher level of being.

Ego

Ego is a state of consciousness wherein the Soul forgets its true nature and identifies with the body, mind, and senses.

Ego is the pseudo Soul, the individualized consciousness of the Soul under the spell of delusion. Ego keeps the Soul Consciousness engaged with sensory activities and overshadows the nature of the Inner Self. It pulls the attention of the Soul outward to the world. It acquires likes, dislikes, attachments, cravings, and needs. It is characterized by a sense of separateness; a primary loneliness which creates subtle melancholy and a deep sense of personal inadequacy—a sense that there is something wrong, something missing. It is a nagging incompleteness that seeks abatement in power, relationships, paranormal experiences, grand accomplishments, and visions of grandeur for the evolution of the race. The ego uses anything, no matter how base or noble, to focus the attention on the tempting promises of fulfillment, completion, and perfection in a world limited, imperfect, and ephemeral by its very nature. It promises the ocean in a desert.

The ego is like a layer of soot covering a magnificent stained glass window. It obstructs the bright sunlight of Divinity that naturally shines through and gives life to our individual persona. It gives us a painful sense of separation from our Source and detracts from the fullness of Life.

The mystical path transcends
the ego's frantic desire to create and
find completeness in a separate personal reality

It brings the Soul to its destiny—
to know and become one
with the absolute fullness of Ultimate Reality

The Highest Meaning and Purpose of Life

A noble life
is not measured by the breadth of what we do
but by the depth of our Realization
of who we truly are

Ultimately, what we have come to do is to unite with God in Mystical Union. We cannot create the Kingdom of Heaven on earth until it is first and fully realized within. The Kingdom of Heaven on earth is most clearly understood as the "effect" of humanity reaching its potential in God Realization. Saving the world and losing one's Soul is a tragic misunderstanding of the Divine Plan. It is truly "putting the cart before the horse." We each are entrusted with a "sacred mission" during this incarnation on the earth plane, and it is to "be perfect as the Father in Heaven is perfect." In other words, know yourself in the fullness and completion of union with God. Know yourself as Pure Spirit.

Chapter Two

Where Am I Going?

Consciousness

Consciousness is the degree to which Essence is reflected in form.

Let's use a loose analogy here. In our solar system the sun is self-luminous fullness itself. It is a perfect luminary. Its essence is light. The moon has no light of its own. Its form is matter. When we see a "dark" moon, there is no light reflected by the sun. There is no correspondence between light and dark. The moon does not reflect the sun so consciousness is considered "low." However, during the full moon there is a complete reflection of the light of the sun onto the surface of the moon. Consciousness is "high" and the moon is resplendent in the fulfillment of its function to illumine the night sky. The moon is a complete reflection of its source, the sun.

Likewise, a human being in the spiritually unconscious state of ego is like a dark moon. A human being in the state of Divine Union is like a full moon.

Consciousness refers to our identity in Source
Intelligence refers to the understanding of creation

Consciousness is described in terms of "states." Each state marks a point of personal identity and provides a certain perspective of reality...of who we are and of what we have the potential to realize. As consciousness becomes fuller, we experience finer and finer, more subtle states of creation until we reach the realms of the Soul, the Creator, the Creator within creation, and God beyond creation. We traverse all aspects of relativity and eventually come home to Ultimate Reality—the essence of our being before manifestation and beyond manifestation.

Seven States of Consciousness

An Overview

Ego (excitation)	**Sleeping** **Dreaming** **Waking/Paranormal**
Soul (Silence)	**Transcendent**
God (ecstasy)	**Creator (Source of manifestation)** **Universal (Creator within Creation)** **Cosmic (God beyond Creation)**

Three Identities

How we experience our identity parallels the state of consciousness that we reflect.

Our identity is our spiritual center of gravity, our point of reference. Who we experience ourselves to be, our point of identity, reflects our consciousness, perspective, beliefs, attitudes, values, emotions, and sense of well-being. It is the experiential answer to the question "Who Am I?" Although we can all recite the book that says we are all God, until the experience of being one with God is our permanent state there is some element of enlightenment but not true God Realization.

1. Outer Self – the Ego

The ego experiences the following to be true:

> I am the body, mind, and senses existing in the multidimensional realms of feeling, thoughts, energy, matter, and light.
>
> I am in the world, am overshadowed by it, and must create my personal reality. I am in a state of incompleteness.
>
> I am separate.
> I am the doer.
> I am imperfect.

The underlying feeling tones are anxiety, fear, overshadowing desire, anger, melancholy, criticalness, and loneliness. A deep sense of "I am not good enough. Something is missing. Somehow I have failed. I am separated from something I want to be united to." The ego can even feel loneliness in intimacy. There is a hole in the heart, the core of one's being, that nothing short of the direct experience of God can ever fill.

2. Inner Self – the Soul

When we experience ourselves as the Soul, we experience ourselves as individualized aspects of Spirit. Our experience is an inner fullness, an inner silence that is not overshadowed by outer circumstances. It is living in the State of Grace from the permanent states of Love, Peace, Wisdom, and Joy (Bliss). It is a sense of self-sufficient completion. It is the source of all right action and thought and the source of noble human virtues. In this state we are perfect instruments of the Divine Will. All of our activity uplifts all of creation.

The Soul is indeed the silent witness to the activity of the body, mind, senses, and ego.

> We are self-sufficient—complete.
> We are in the world but not of the world,
> Living as silent witnesses in the State of Grace.

> **"The Kingdom of Heaven is within."** [5]

3. Supreme Self – God

From the first realization of the Divine to the final experience of existence beyond duality, there are the three progressions and states of God Realization:

> I am one with Spirit (God) as the Creator
> (God Consciousness)

> I am one with Spirit (God) within Creation
> (Unity Consciousness/Christ Consciousness)

> I am one with Spirit (God)
> outside of Its Creation
> (Cosmic Consciousness)

Here, in Cosmic Consciousness, there is a complete paradigm shift. Our experience of reality is now the living knowledge that:

> There is only Consciousness.
> There is only one Doer.
> Everything is perfect.

We live in the state of Ecstatic Union. This is seeing reality from the viewpoint of Ultimate Reality. This is true wisdom—seeing the finite from the eyes of the Infinite.

The Three Ego States – Outer Self

The sleeping, dreaming, and waking (normal and paranormal) states are each unique.

In deep sleep the ego is dissolved and rests in the Silence of the Soul. This state is healing and refreshing. The mind gets sorely needed rest, and the body becomes more normalized and rebalanced and starts the process of healing. Many people have used deep, undisturbed sleep to heal the traumas of stress, certain mental illnesses, and deep body fatigue. When in this state, we are not aware that we are not aware.

Dreaming is the state of the subconscious mind processing impressions from the present and the past. Dreams can often reflect states just underneath the level of conscious awareness. Often when we dream, we are aware of our dreaming. In it we can create worlds populated with people, places, events, and life forms that amuse, frighten, and enchant us. Dreams reflect our physical, mental, and psychological states. Seldom are they prophetic, but they do have significance. They reflect the condition of the waves on the waters of stillness, the quality and activity of the mind as it creates ripples on the smooth surface pond of our Inner Being. Dreams are the sum-total reflection of how we process stimuli as it enters our nervous system during waking consciousness. Dreams are a view into the contents of the subconscious.

The waking state is a simple state of perceiving stimuli through the central nervous system, identifying these stimuli, feeling their effects in the physiology (emotions), categorizing them (fitting them into our belief system), and deciding what to act on and what to let slip effortlessly into our subconscious minds. This is the domain of the conscious mind governed by logic, reason, feeling, and desire.

The paranormal state is the experience of thoughts, impressions, feelings, visions, and intuition from one or more subtle states of creation that are for the most part non-physical. For the last several hundred years, with the advent of spiritualism (communing with the "other side"), *the meaning of true spirituality has been diluted to include that which, by definition, it transcends.* Spirituality is moving to the Source or Essence of Being, which is Spirit Unmanifest, and not Spirit clothed in another subtle state of creation. Paranormal powers are not exhibits of spiritual advancement. Although many great saints and sages may exhibit some of these powers, the ability to exhibit these powers does not make one a great saint. These powers reflect sensitivity and the ability to tune into realms that are invisible to the five senses. These realms are subtle and for the most part are hidden, yet they are still realms and belong to the laws of duality. They are of form and not Essence.

Today's "metaphysical" or "paranormal" accomplishments include contacting the departed ones on the other side, the notion of receiving messages from beings located in other realms of creation, proclaimed intuitive "insights" into the condition of an individual's "spiritual" and physical health, seeing visions, balancing energy and energy centers, "getting" prophetic impressions and prophecies of major changes in world conditions and consciousness from so-called "highly evolved life

forms from other planets and dimensions," channeling, communing with UFO inhabitants, communicating with crystal structures
for historical insight and future happenings—virtually anything
an active, imaginative, subtle mind can receive when it reflects
on these "spaces of multidimensional stimuli." Even the urgent
quest to unite with "light bodies" is still seeking another form of
form, a body. It is getting side-tracked by another diversion.
The point of discrimination here is that in the paranormal and
metaphysical realms, the focus is still on "realm" and "body."
The true meaning of Mystical Spirituality refers to the First
Cause and not a secondary effect; Ultimate Reality, not "other
realities" or personal reality. Spirituality is not stuck in the
attempt to understand metaphysics or the nature of the "toys,"
nor does it eschew this knowledge. Knowledge of the secular is
knowledge of the secular and is no substitute for God Realization.

"For what does it profit a man if he gains
the whole world
and loses his Soul?"[6]

**Of all the ego states of consciousness, the paranormal is the
most tempting and can easily distract a Soul from its spiritual destiny—union with God.** The "toys" can be so tempting
and can cause us to lose sight of the Toy Maker! And the ego/
mind is so tricky—it calls this diversion into the paranormal
"spiritual."

In the ego state we are identified as body, mind, and senses. Emotions and events can overshadow us. There is a sense of separateness that enlivens our desires. We substitute the pursuit of ephemeral happiness (which must have an object) for the unchanging Joy, which is our inner nature. This Joy we already have. However, we crave completion and seek ultimate fulfillment in human relationships which cannot possibly bear the burden of what we truly seek—Divine Relationship. We seek power and control to gain pleasure and avoid pain, and we focus our attention looking outward to create a "heaven on earth" while missing the **"Seek first the Kingdom of Heaven within."**[7] "Heaven on earth" is a secondary gain of individual God Realization. Even focusing on such a noble goal as evolution of the species can be a diversion from the primary mission of attaining Divine Union.

The primary characteristic of this ego state is excitation of the mind and senses. The ego doesn't know to "go within" and resists it by looking for diversions elsewhere.

The State of the Soul – Inner Self

The Soul is found in Inner Silence. It is the Silent Witness of outer focus and activity. Its nature is Love, Peace, Wisdom, and Joy. It is God within us, an immortal reflection of the Supreme Self. It is awareness without an object of awareness, pure awareness experiencing itself as ineffable equanimity and grace. It is the silent observer of our waking, dreaming, sleeping, and paranormal states.

As knowledge and temporary happiness
are found in outer excitation,
Love, Peace, Wisdom, and Joy
are our natural states in Silence

The Soul's Peace is an unbounded sense
of well-being, faith, and surrender
to the perfection of God Within,
an equanimity that is never overshadowed
by the continuous modulation of duality

When in communion with our Soul,
every act, thought, word, and deed
that moves through our being is an act of love

Today love is defined is as series of conditioned responses to life's circumstances and events that can be learned and evaluated by the mind in ego consciousness. The "spirit" of love has been lost to the "letter" of attitude and actions. However, real love, the full expression of the essence of Love, cannot be determined by a fixed set of behaviors. Love is a state of consciousness that flows naturally from communion with the Inner Self, Soul. Consider the life of Christ. Christ lived from the essence of Love and His Love took many diverse and apparent contradictory forms, from scourging the money changers in the temple and calling the "holy men" of the day hypocrites and brood of vipers, to healing the sick, raising the dead, and sacrificing His life on a cross.

> **Love is not an absolute behavior or a feeling or set of prescriptions or proscriptions; it is a state of consciousness, a commitment to the highest good, and to the action most appropriate for the highest good of evolution at that moment. It is the force of evolution and a spontaneous response that brings all of life to a higher level of being. There will be as many determinations of the highest good as there are people in different states of consciousness. One's state of consciousness will dictate perspective and the wisdom to discriminate and act.**

Being grounded in the state of the Inner Self allows us to fully live and participate in the world without being overshadowed and caught up in it.

In the world, but not of the world

The individual's first accomplishment is communion with the Soul. In this state, the State of Grace, all suffering ceases. We are connected to the Peace, Love, Security, and Fulfillment of our Inner Self. There is the experience of being connected with both the inner aspect of the Soul and the outer aspect of the body, mind, and senses. We are completely engaged in events and things but are also aware of that deep, undisturbed internal peace so that we seem to be "witnessing these things." We are full and "in bliss" for no apparent external reason. Whatever comes—ups or downs, sickness or health, poverty or abundance, or any of duality's opposites—there is an abiding sense of equanimity and ever-new Joy. The outer and the inner are in perfect balance and harmony. Nothing can disturb this state once it has been stabilized. It is like being in a movie theater and realizing that you are no longer tossed and turned by the frames of pictures playing on the movie screen. You begin to realize that you are the pure, non-changing, self-fulfilled field (screen) upon which the motion pictures of life (karmas) are playing themselves out. Then you can really enjoy the movie and begin to get a glimpse that this is not as real as it seems to be.

The primary characteristics of this state are deep, imperturbable Inner Peace, Joy, Love, Wisdom, and self-sufficiency. When in this state, all thought and action are governed by the ideal principles of Love, Peace, Wisdom, and Joy. These principles cannot be learned by the ego state's mind and mental processes. They flow naturally from communion with the Soul.

Consciousness identifying with
the mental waves of change
is restlessness

Consciousness identifying with
Changelessness
is Peace

The Supreme Self –
God Consciousness

God Consciousness is the first state of God Realization. It is the perception of Spirit as the Creator and Source of the Soul. It is the state of the Soul merging with its Source.

Excitation characterizes the ego states

Silence characterizes the state of the Soul

Ecstasy characterizes the states of

God Communion

This is the realization of our being one with God as the Creator. This is the experience of the "saint," no matter what religion or creed. For those whose temperament is more of the intellect and who aspire to the path of knowledge, this experience is one of great awe, majesty, and illumination. For others, there is a deep sense of "falling in love" with God. The experience is that of profound devotion: the Divine marriage of Soul and its Source. For others, this inspires a great sense of service and wanting to spread this Joy of Divine Communion through service, alleviating human suffering, and religious endeavor. None of these modes of experience is exclusive of the other and they all overlap with one or the other being the most prevalent. These different means of expressing God Realization are simply due to the variation in temperament.

The primary characteristic of this state is a joyous sense of ecstasy.

Universal Consciousness – Christ Consciousness

This is the experience of God within creation.

In this state there is a vast sense of fullness. This is the home of miracles. The Consciousness of God within creation is called Unity or Christ Consciousness. The God-Realized one feels his presence everywhere in creation: in every atom, in every galaxy, in every being. He is one with the laws of nature. All powers are at his disposal, from materializing objects to healing, to raising the dead. All knowledge is available and every action is in perfect accord with the Divine Plan. He has transcended the limitations of time, space, mind, and the three bodies: physical, astral, and etheric (light). The universe is his body and all things that happen in the universe are his sensations.

At this point the Soul participates further in the nature of God and can demonstrate the absolute Divine qualities of Omniscience, Omnipotence, Omnipresence—and can spontaneously heal, alleviate karma, and change the consciousness of those who attune themselves to him.

The primary characteristics of this state are Omniscience, Omnipotence, Omnipresence, unbounded Love, and complete control over the laws of nature.

Cosmic Consciousness

This is the experience of God beyond creation.

Words cannot bear the burden of describing this state. The great ones do tell us that in this state we dream the cosmic dream of creation with the Master Dramatist Himself. We have reached our Home, our final destiny, and the point from which we have come. We have fulfilled our obligation to go forth, experience and be all that we can be, know ourselves as the Soul, and merge the Soul with its Source without losing our sense of individuality—and watch the great play of creation from the state of Ultimate Reality.

The primary characteristic of this state is that we live beyond the dream of duality while fully participating in whatever station of life has been assigned to us in the form of our earthly duties and responsibilities. Many who have achieved this state have lived in obscurity as productive householders, taking care of family and other "mundane" necessities. Their great "world mission" was achieved in **who** they became, not in what they did. The subtle influence of their powerful consciousness was a force of evolution far surpassing the efforts of outer social reform.

Summary of the States of Consciousness[8]

Outer Self – Ego Consciousness

Sleeping, dreaming, waking, and paranormal states.
Sense of separation.
Metaphysical understanding.

Excitation

Inner Self – Soul Consciousness

Peace, Love, Joy, and Wisdom.
Silent Witness.

Silence

God Consciousness

The perception of Spirit as creator—the Soul merged with the God.

Communion

Universal Consciousness

The experience of God within creation. We experience the awareness, intelligence, and form of the universe as our awareness, intelligence, and form.

Union

Cosmic Consciousness

The experience of God beyond the dream of creation.

Transcendence

The Three Points of Identity

Point of Identity	State of Consciousness	Mode	Feeling Tone	Perspective
Ego	Waking Sleeping Dreaming Paranormal	**Control**	**Excitation**	I am separate I am the doer I am imperfect
	My will be done...			In duality
Soul	Peace Love Joy Wisdom	**Surrender**	**Silence**	The Kingdom of Heaven is within
	Thy will be done...			In world but not of it
God	Omniscience Omnipotence Omnipresence All-Loving	**Merging**	**Ecstasy**	"I and the Father are One."
	God is living Its life through us.			Beyond duality

Chapter Three

How Do I Get There?

The Spiritual Path

The spiritual path is a process of allowing God to live Its Life through us.

The spiritual path whose destination is Union with Ultimate Reality is a progressive broadening of consciousness, perspective, and identity, as well as a corresponding development of character and noble personal qualities.

The sole activity of the spiritual life is to allow the higher states of consciousness which are our true nature to be realized and expressed in our everyday life. It is not a struggle, but a gentle process of receptivity. The primary technique is to focus our attention inward on God while living fully in activity.

The path that we follow corresponds to our highest concept of our destination on the path to God Realization.

Our idea of God is a jumping-off point and not an end point. This idea evolves as we experience more fully the nature of God in the various states of spiritual consciousness.

Discrimination

Once a great saint was asked what quality is the most important one to develop on the path to God. His reply was "discrimination."

> **There are many paths called spiritual paths, but they do not all get you to the same place. Only the paths that take you to God will get you to God. Other paths have other destinations: the evolution of the race, learning "lessons," developing paranormal powers, service to humanity, learning certain "loving" attitudes and behaviors, moving "energy," perfect health, and so on.**
>
> **The primary aspect of discrimination is to continuously ask oneself, "Does this get me closer to my goal of union with God, or not?"**

The Five Paradigms

There seem to be five general answers to the question, "Where Am I Going?" They are reflected in the five primary paradigms of life: hedonism, metaphysics, humanitarianism, religion, and mysticism. Each one parallels a sense of the highest purpose we can conceive of for our life at that time. There are times when we move from one paradigm to another, usually in ascending order, although there are no absolute lines of demarcation, especially with the first three.

People question when or whether they should change paradigms. It is usually not a matter of *should*. It comes down to what we want. We are usually where we need to be at the time (but not for all time). It is a matter of whether or not the paradigm is working for us. If it is not working anymore, then we move. The object here is to eventually get off of the cycle of birth and death—to live beyond duality. And when we are living beyond duality, even while being in it, we transform and raise the "vibration" of all life around us! One God-Realized Soul does more for the world than an army of committed volunteers. Changing conditions without also changing the consciousness that leads to the conditions is futile.

Hedonism is the focus of service to the self

Its primary objective is to gain pleasure and avoid pain. It craves all the things of the world that promise fulfillment, power, prestige, and sensation. "Every man for himself."

It is the wave on the ocean primarily concerned for itself.

Metaphysics is the focus on understanding and control of vibratory creation

Here we take possession of the Creator's "toys." The concern is for knowledge of and control of the laws of nature—energy and light. The concept of evolution for the human race and the planet is foremost. It defines things "spiritual" as things unseen and more subtle than what can be perceived by the five senses. It is the realm of the paranormal and is concerned with the exploration of the nature and relationship of the three realms that constitute duality: physical, astral, and etheric. It gives supremacy to the mind/ego, assigning it the absolute powers and absolute responsibility for creating personal "reality." It is about "my will be done."

It is the wave on the ocean using the power of the ocean to sculpt its experience.

Humanitarianism is the focus on the "other"

This marks a transition in the ego's preoccupation with itself and its penchant for control and comfort to an expression of love—a concern for the welfare of all beings. Service to the "other" is an essential aspect of the spiritual path leading to Unity with God. It moves the point of attention to something beyond the individual mind/ego and individual "personal reality." It is a profound means of purification and lessening the vice-grip hold of the ego.

It is the wave on the ocean dedicating itself to the well-being of all the other waves.

Religion leads us back to our Source

Religion means to "lead back" to God. Pure religion does exactly that. Saints and sages of all traditions are living witnesses to this fact. Pure religion is a means of bringing us to the direct experience of the God within ourselves, and to the vision of God within and beyond His creation. It leads to the communion of the Soul with its Source. It is "Thy Will be done."

It is the wave on the ocean in loving relationship to its source —the ocean itself.

Mysticism is merging with God and living outside the dream of duality

Mystical Spirituality is beyond the mind's capability to fathom. It is truly a "mystery." Mystical Union is the ultimate goal of spirituality. It is being one with God beyond creation, viewing creation as a dream with only One Actor dreaming it is many, only One Doer dreaming that the many are acting independently. It is complete Perfection within the dream of imperfection.

This is the wave on the ocean merging back into its Source— without losing its sense of pure individuality. The wave merges again with the ocean as full, complete, and differentiated.

The wave merges into the ocean such that the ocean never forgets the experience of having been the wave. (This is the essence of the mystical experience.)

Hedonism – our ego selves possess us

Metaphysics – we try to understand and control
creation

Humanitarianism – we give ourselves for others

Religion – we possess God in relationship

Mysticism – God possesses us as His very Own Self

We can spend this lifetime
getting to know ourselves
(which we lose at death)
or getting to know God
(which we keep for Eternity)

Descent to Matter

The act of creation is a repulsion from Source.

On the vast ocean of Silence, Consciousness stirs. The modulations of Consciousness condense to form fine structures of intelligence and impulse, which progressively condense to grosser and denser layers of thought, form, and matter. It is like water condensing into ice. Spirit condenses into individualized Soul aspects, which inhabit vehicles or bodies of thought, feeling, and sense. The Soul forgets its nature and identifies with the material vehicles. There is a sense of separation and ego is formed. This ego becomes subject to the cosmic laws of cause and effect (karma). Its focus is outward and it desperately seeks to control the circumstances of its existence to avoid pain and find comfort. The ego begins a complex and never-ending task of developing a "self" with a keen sense of wants, needs, and desires that will never be fulfilled.

As the life force flows down and out, driven by the power of overshadowing desire, Soul Consciousness is lost to various states of body consciousness—whether gross or subtle bodies. The Soul is charmed and deluded by material creation. The story of Adam and Eve here is so appropriate. They embraced duality when they ate (took their "life nourishment" or understanding) from the tree of the limited knowledge of relative creation and forgot their Divine Nature. They became bound by the polarities of relativity and knew suffering—separation from their original state.

Although there is only one Universal Power, it has two very distinct directions. The first is the repulsion from Source, the force of projection out from the Unmanifest Consciousness of God. This going out produces the many manifest forms of the universe—God Consciousness modulating down to the frozen thickness of matter. The second force inherent in creation is that of Love, which is the primal attraction that brings everything back to the source of God Consciousness. This power of Love is stronger than the power of creation. It transcends law and karma. It melts the frozen separateness of mind/ego.

The ocean waters of pure Spirit form into a multiplicity of frozen entities of individualized "cubes" of ice which feel separate, alone, inadequate and somehow outside of their Source, forgetting their oneness with the vast ocean of Being. This is the play of creation.

Love is attraction back to Source—
Seeking Wholeness

Ascent to Source

The Mystical Spiritual path is a reversal of the creation process. The spiritual process is about waking from the dream of creation and going beyond duality. It is realizing the higher states of consciousness that reflect our true nature. It is an effortless "allowing" of these states to be known, yet it requires "self effort" in the form of spiritual practices to gently cultivate the necessary "receptivity." (All things in duality are expressed in paradox!)

It is getting off the cycle of birth and death. At some point, either from inspiration or desperation, the individual realizes that what he has been looking for is not "out there" for him and that the means to attain it are not working. He begins the spiritual journey through an act of surrender and starts the process of "unselfing" the complex ego with its overshadowing desires, likes, dislikes, ideas of "how it should be," and its adamant refusal to submit its will to anything beyond itself.

The individual and separate entity of ice melts back into the vast waters of Spirit in such as way that the Divine Ocean always remembers the experience of having been that individual cube of ice.

On the spiritual path that leads to Union with God:

Grace replaces karma

Love transcends law

and Spirit attracts Itself to Itself

Spirit attracting Itself back to Itself

is the role of God of revealing Himself to us

Experience of the Descent to Matter

Spirit takes form and begins the descent into vibratory creation (matter) to create a "self," which it experiences as its reality:

Law (Karma)
Control
Desire
Suffering
Excitation

Law (Karma)

When being drawn into creation and functioning from the ego state, all Souls must abide by the laws of cause and effect, or karma. Karma is the predisposition for us to experience our personal life circumstances based on the sum-total of all our thoughts, deeds, actions, desires, cravings, and dreams.

The origin of karma is thought and action originating in ego consciousness. It is desire that overshadows our true nature; it is our human understanding bound in "ignorance." All action performed in ego consciousness is out of balance; the correction of this imbalance is karma.

The primary desire that overshadows us is the desire for the fruits of our actions, to get what we want and to take responsibility for getting it. It is the craving of the human, in ignorance, to be attached to results of his actions and to take responsibility for what is not his responsibility. From a higher state of Soul Consciousness we realize that we are responsible for what we do, but not necessarily the result of our actions. From the state of Ultimate Reality we realize that there is only God and God is the sole Doer. The "dream" is that we think we are separate and we are doing it all on our own.

However, there are four spiritual virtues (attitudes) that help mitigate the sting of karma. They are surrender, faith, patience, and self-acceptance.

Surrender tells us to know what we can and can't do. We do our part—and then let go!

Faith tells us that there is a higher plan that the human mind cannot fathom. We do what we can and leave the results up to God. Life and existence is not a snapshot but an eternal movie. Ultimately, everything we experience comes from God to in some way help us find our way back "Home."

Patience tells us that everything has a season—no matter how hard we try, things have cycles. An old Celtic saying tells us that "no matter how many women you put on the job, it still takes nine months to make a baby." And whether these actions and results we seek are good actions or bad actions, causing good karma or bad karma, is immaterial. It does not matter whether we are bound by an iron chain or bound by a gold chain. Bondage is bondage.

Knowledge can describe the meal
but only as a menu!
It can't give you the direct experience!

Self-acceptance is being comfortable with ourselves and we can't be comfortable knowing only half of ourselves. This self-acceptance cannot fully happen until the self is whole and balanced. It is the natural outcome of realization of both the inner and outer. It is the outcome of the State of Grace, the state of Soul Consciousness, in which we live from the qualities of the Soul—Love, Peace, Wisdom, and Joy—forever transcending the ego nature of overshadowing desire, greed, control, and inadequacy. Until the inner and outer selves merge, like two wings on one bird, self-acceptance is knowing that we are a work in progress right now, this very instant—that everything that happened had to happen in just that way for us to be at the point of growth where we are today. We are being sculpted by the Divine Sculpture. Our completion cannot come solely from our own efforts, but also by God's Grace. Our perfection will come when it comes. We can only use effort to be receptive. Self effort can only take us so far. It can lead us to a place of great receptivity for God to do His work within us and to reveal Himself to us. Our job is to be receptive to the work of God within us through the practice of surrender, faith, patience, and self-acceptance.

In Mystical Spirituality it is not a matter
of possessing God,
but allowing God to possess us

A higher understanding of karma goes beyond the notion of tit for tat, or an eye for an eye. There are certain circumstances that we allow to occur in our lives for our growth and development. Sometimes we will experience a sickness that we may have "agreed to" before we were even born into this body. It is popular and simplistic to think that we created a particular illness and everything else that happens to us moment by moment (this is evidence of the ego's desperate need for control). However, most of the time what we experience is something we "agreed to" experience, or have "allowed" to be a part of our lives, for a much bigger purpose that has to do with our Journey Home.

Yes, in a sense, we do create our own reality, but our current reality is the product of forces set into motion many, many, many lifetimes ago. The human mind can never fully understand causality of the present. On this, both mysticism and physics agree.

A simple but effective way to understand karma is to understand that every life has an after life, every thought has an after thought, and every action has an after action. Karma is the compensation or correction mechanism to create balance when we have gone "off course." If you had a sail boat and decided to set sail from New York to Liverpool, you would generally head in an easterly direction. Without having exact course coordinates (Soul Consciousness), you would end up somewhere between Iceland and South Africa, but probably not in Liverpool. To prevent this complete waste of a trip, karma is the universal law of cause and effect, predispositions and circumstances, that corrects our course in a compensatory fashion so that when we are in "ignorance" of our true nature (true course) the winds of karma blow us back to the "right" or "left" as necessary to create a course correction. After enough "tacking" and getting buffeted in the great Atlantic storms of correction, we seek to find our true bearings, set a true course, and find safe harbor at our destination: we find a spiritual path that leads us to our Source.

When we steer the boat one way or the other without Soul communion, no matter how noble our intentions, we can never be wholly on the mark and thus need the winds of karma to rebalance our progress. This compass is within, not in mere "human intuition," but in Soul communion. The markers at sea continuously change and are often a mirage. "Seek first the Kingdom of Heaven, and all else shall be added unto you." [9]

Control

Control is fear in action, a reflection of the ego's need for security in an ever-changing duality.

There is always some need for reasonable control over one's circumstances. If rent is due and you have no money, it is reasonable to get a job. Spirituality is, indeed, practicality at all levels!

However, by nature the ego feels a fundamental loneliness and an underlying fear stemming from a sense of separation from Source. Although the mind cannot tell us about God, because the mind cannot know that which transcends it, God can be known by the heart. The heart is the core of one's being—the seat of the Soul. However, the ego uses the limited mind to try to make sense of life and find its place in the greater scheme of things. Whatever seeming truth it may arrive at, that truth is inadequate to understand that there is a grand and loving Being whose Will is being perfectly played out in this seemingly "imperfect" world. **The ego carries with it three primary illusions that are gradually dispelled as the Soul journeys back to God. They are: I am separate. I am the doer. I am imperfect.** This is our "reality" when we are in the ego state.

Truth is understood differently in different states of consciousness

Although the ego is fundamentally innocent, it feels great responsibility for its state and the state of things in general. The ego did not create this state. It is God's dream (see "The Bigger, Bigger Picture" on page 148). It was set up so that the Lord would conceal Himself and the Soul would identify with the body, mind, and senses. This is part of God's sport (lila). *It is also set up so that God would fulfill His plan for creation, which is for the Absolute to experience limitation and then find its Infinite nature within the finite.* This understanding is at the core of Mystical Spirituality. The ego did nothing wrong. Yes, it is looking in the wrong direction and is temporarily lost, looking for love and fulfillment in all the wrong places, but the final role of God is that He will reveal Himself to us. And so the urge for something better and greater is the Divine Impulse within that keeps us moving through the Decent and Ascent until we reach our goal. This desire for something better takes form progressively in terms of our paradigm. From hedonism to mysticism, these systems, these paradigms, are innocent, necessary, and profoundly beautiful steps on the ladder to complete Self Realization. When we take this perspective and see the hedonism around us, there is less of a "pinch" because we understand that these Souls, as all Souls, are in fact on the journey home. And eventually all the pain and suffering that the ego inevitably causes will spurn these Souls to greater questioning and understanding of their Divine human potential.

So with great compassion, it is natural for the poor ego to try to reconcile this colossal misunderstanding—I am separate, I am the doer, I am imperfect—by trying to take control over its environment and resist with all possible force the inevitable changes and transformations that occur while on the earth plane.

Ultimately, there is only One Consciousness, One Doer, and Everything Is Perfect. This is true in Mystical Union, but (and this is very important) it would be inappropriate for us to act as if we were in that state when we are actually in another. We must act from the state we are in, yet take comfort in the knowledge that there is a much bigger Truth that we are growing into, a Truth that is sweet, gentle, complete, ecstatic, and all loving.

The plan for creation is for the Unbounded
to experience limitation

and find Its Unbounded Nature
while experiencing finite creation

Desire

**Overshadowing desire is the human attempt to substitute
the limited ephemeral pleasures of the world for unbounded
Spiritual Bliss. It is the result of not experiencing the fullness
of Soul communion.**

The desire to know, love, serve, and eventually merge with God
in Mystical Union is what makes man in truth "the capacity for
God." Some say that on the spiritual path we must eliminate
our desire nature. However, if you look closely at what they are
really saying, they are telling us that we must not be controlled
by our cravings or those desires that overshadow our primary
desire to be One with God.

On the later stages of the spiritual path, the great saints and
God-Realized Beings have no real desires. God takes care of
every need—every moment they are the living expression of
Divine Will. They are living proof of the great spiritual law:

"Seek first the Kingdom of Heaven
And all else shall be added unto you."[10]

Most of us who live in the world have healthy desires to provide for our families, share our experiences, make the world a
better place, and live in safety. These desires are important
and we should work toward fulfilling them. The problem arises
when we become overshadowed by them so that our time,
attention, and energy is solely dedicated to attaining them.
Other desires for things, such as fame, fortune, power, and ultimate fulfillment in human relationship are attempts to fill in the
inner emptiness, the gaps within us that are left by the absence
of the presence of God within.

The desire to love God
is the fulfillment of all desires

Suffering

Suffering is the natural consequence of our ego's experience of separation from God and our Inner Self.

Suffering occurs when we become overshadowed by externals and lose our sense of security, purpose, and connection to the greater whole. It is living outside Unity as a separate entity bound by the karmic laws and consequences of thoughts, deeds, and feelings that are alien to this Oneness. Pain on this earth plane is part of having a body and all that goes with the extreme paradox of being pure Spirit locked in a small human form with needs, desires, and cravings inherited from its primitive physical and psychological nature. Pain is inevitable but suffering is not. Suffering does not have to be a part of our earth experience.

Much suffering is due to a distorted idea of control and the subsequent lack of faith. Suffering is perpetuated by the overshadowing belief that what is happening "should not" be happening that way. Suffering is the result of holding on to a fixed idea of how things in duality "should" be. It is expecting perfection where it cannot be found. **Faith is knowing deeply that whatever is coming to us is coming to us from God for a higher purpose than what the limited human mind can understand.**

There Is Only One True Beloved

"The human heart has a Beloved, its first and only Love, and He is the object of its desire. We are seeking Him in all our seeking even when we betray Him, substituting for Him the myriad beauties of creation, which He has set on our path to point us to Him and kindle desire.

"We bear within our very substance an open wound of longing, dissatisfaction. We experience this but most often do not recognize its cause. We seek to assuage our wound in one way or another but there is no healing of it apart from Him. It is a blessed thing to suffer from this wound and the greater the pain, the greater the blessedness when we know Him." [11]

Often this suffering of separation begins the process of surrender, a process that leads through grace to joyous alignment to the Will of God. It is the diminishing of the false sense of control that keeps the ego focused on the external life, continually seeking ultimate fulfillment through human relationships, comforts, thrilling visions, paranormal excitements, and the promise of a "kingdom of heaven" without.

*"O you who were created for union of love with
God Himself and whom He is ever attracting to
Himself, what are you doing with your precious
life, with your time? You are laboring for
nothingness and all you think you possess is pure
misery. O terrible human blindness. So great a
light about you and you do not see it! So clear a
voice sounding and you do not hear!"* [12]

Each of us by the very fact of being human is made for union
with God. We must choose to develop it and allow God to
develop it. We must wake up and seek Him where He is—that
is, within ourselves.

*"O most beautiful of creatures, transcendent
spirit, who long to know where your Beloved is
and where you may find Him so as to be united
with Him. He dwells within you. You are
yourself the tabernacle, His secret hiding place.
Rejoice, exult, for all you could possibly desire, all
your heart's longing is so close, so intimate as to
be within you; you cannot be without Him."* [13]

Silence and Excitation

Silence is the home of God in creation.

It is the inner "witness" of individual existence. It is our true nature and characterizes the nature and quality of the Soul.

Silence is a subtle, quiet inner state, which is the true home of the State of Grace, most often characterized as the states of Peace, Love, Wisdom, and Joy. It is the pure state of the Soul.

This Silence is the home of the perfect blueprint of what and who we have the potential to be. Accessing the Silence within and cultivating it in daily life will allow us to spontaneously express Love, Peace, Wisdom and Joy, while diminishing the subconscious impressions and consequent attitudes and behaviors that we strive so diligently to "work on." In Silence resides all of our noble qualities and our full potential. Cultivating the Silence within brings forth without effort virtue, joy, grace, and who we have the potential to become.

Silence naturally heals the mind and restructures our consciousness.

Excitation is the noisy, mentally agitated state covering over the state of Silence. It is the state of ego.

Higher states of consciousness come from nurturing the Silence. This conscious nurturing is called "living a contemplative life," and it is available to busy householders as "silence in activity."

Sometimes people mistake Silence for the absence of speech. The mind can be active and excited when you are not speaking. Not talking and just walking in the woods is not the same as Inner Silence. Yet, on the other hand, you can be mingling with the crowds, answering the telephone, and doing a demanding job in the world—all from the Inner State of Silence. The proof positive of Inner Silence is when you can feel everything there is to feel and do and see in the world around you but not be overshadowed by it, not lose your inner state for one second. Inner Silence is like the pure white movie screen upon which the dramas of life are played. The show must go on as it will, but the Silent screen is not altered or affected.

Silence is the means of
restructuring our consciousness

The Experience of the Ascent to Ultimate Reality

As the Soul seeks to unite to its Source, it begins the process of Ascent, and during that process it experiences as its reality:

Silence

Attraction to God

Unselfing

Renunciation

Purification

Surrender

Faith

Knowing God

Patience

Self-acceptance

Love

Grace

God's Will

Wisdom

Virtue

Truth

Joy

Attraction to God

What pulls us to God? God's longing for us. His Love, His desire to draw us to Himself and give us Himself, is ultimately greater than any desire we may have. Love is the power and force of the One attracting us to wholeness with Him, the One again. Love is the relationship to the wholeness of someone or something. We can trust His longing for us. He awaits only our willingness. **We cannot reach Him solely by our own efforts. Our responsibility is to be receptive to Him, be receptive to the "Word" working within us.** So the perfect prayer, in the words of St. John of the Cross, is "to stand naked [without desire] before God. And what will God do? God will take possession of us. And is that not the purpose of life?"[14]

Unselfing

The primary task and first step on the Ascent to Source is to empty out the "ego self" and fill the container of our individual being with God.

Even doing spiritual practices, we have to be careful of a deeply rooted self-orientation. When we do spiritual practices to gain something, or have some supernatural experience, we are practicing "spiritual materialism." Mystical Spirituality is a giving of ourselves completely to God in a relationship of love.

And like all love, Love is its own reward and seeks no return or consolation. The desire to love God is the fulfillment of all desires and the primary means of ridding us of the false self, the ego.

God has everything but our love

We may start a spiritual practice to attain some peace and release from certain mental excitations or emotional emptiness, but at the highest level, spiritual practices (no matter what the result) are an act of loving God.

Ultimately, we meditate and do practices not to gain, but to give. God has everything but our love.

Unselfing is replacing self-will with the Will of God. We go from "my will be done" to "Thy Will be done."

Unselfing involves using a meditation and prayer practice, which reverses the flow of energy and attention from down and out into activity through the spiritual chakras, to moving the energy in and up to the higher centers of consciousness.

Unselfing is giving up the notion of an individual truth (ego truth) and embracing transcendental truth through sacred teachings, scriptures, and God-Realized teachers. In a way, it is letting go of much of what we used to think was true and replacing it with the ageless wisdom of the Realized Mystics. This is very difficult for the modern Westerner who is taught the "supremacy of the mind" and the absolute right beyond rights to have "one's own unique truth."

Unselfing is sanctification of the personality wherein the purified persona is an instrument of the Will of God and not held slave to an overshadowing personal will.

The elements of personality to be sanctified were first described by ancient metaphysicians who spoke of the experience of creation using the four elements and their psychological qualities.

1. Fire (will, activity)
2. Earth (structure, alignment)
3. Air (thought, perspective)
4. Water (feeling/relationship)

In the process of spiritualizing material experiences, each of these elements must be sanctified by the virtues of the Soul and used to their greatest potential in elevating human (ego) consciousness.

The ego, also, being the state of separation from its source (the Soul), has four elemental modalities of experience:

1.   Fear
2.   Inadequacy
3.   Control/tension
4.   Greed

For the ego (being that state in which the Soul has forgotten its own identity and is identifying itself with the body, mind and senses, the instruments of experience within material creation) the states of fear, inadequacy, control, tension, and greed are fitting and natural. These are the elements of human suffering and they are the direct result of the great separation (or apparent separation) from God. The ego feels alone in the universe. It may have other relationships and intimacies and yet there is a sense of loneliness as well as a sense of incompleteness in intimate partnerships. There is a sense that something is missing. There is a gentle melancholy and a feeling of being somehow "not good enough." The only available modality is to assume a tremendous sense of responsibility and attempt to control the outer circumstances of life to assuage the inner sense of emptiness. Philosophies of immediate ego gratification are adopted..."you create your own reality here and now!" There emerges a greed for fulfillment and an idea of a utopian "heaven without" that is possible to all who visualize it, will it, and believe it so. Inevitably, that fails. It is too superficial. It does not take into account many, many things.

The four Soul virtues that address the states of the ego and purify them are:

1. Faith, which overcomes fear.

2. Self-acceptance, which replaces inadequacy.

3. Surrender, which alleviates the need for control and the ensuing tension.

4. Patience in the state of fulfillment, which eliminates the angst of greed when in the state of separation or lack of fulfillment.

It is the "religion" of the ego that:

- Usurps the power of the Soul and wrongly directs its efforts to look for fulfillment where fulfillment cannot be found (ultimate fulfillment as "the Kingdom of Heaven" is an inner state of the Soul—Love, Peace, Wisdom, and Joy and not an outer state created by "success," relationships, paranormal powers, etc.)
- Creates a deep sense of tension and overwhelming sense of responsibility for the circumstances and events of our lives (yes, we do create our own reality but we do so over vast eons of time...many experiences today are acts of balance caused by actions and thoughts set into play in a very distant past—our karma)

"Unselfing" is giving up the sense of an absolute personal life and giving one's life completely to God as the wax of a candle burns selflessly in service to the flame.

When we "unself" our self

God becomes our self

There are three primary practices in the process of "unselfing."

Renunciation
Purification
Surrender

May God empty me of everything
but His Presence

Renunciation

Renunciation is letting go of the attachment to anything that is not of Silence. It is giving up what takes us away from our ultimate goal of Mystical Union.

By definition, renunciation is giving a little (that which takes us away from God) to get back a great deal (fulfillment in God Union). In practice, it is giving everything to God. The end point of renunciation is that we are not overshadowed by the circumstances and events of life. We are deeply grounded in the state of Soul Consciousness and are in the world but not of it. It is the spirit in which we fulfill our three primary tasks while journeying on the spiritual path:

Perform our everyday duties as they are set out for us.

Serve the needs and interests of others to the degree we can.

Practice the presence of God within.

For the monastic, renunciation is

the vow of poverty

For the householder, renunciation is

the vow of generosity

The simple attitudinal act of giving everything to God is a subtle and profound moving beyond the selfishness of the ego.

Man seeks to possess. God seeks to give.

Man seeks to possess God. God seeks to possess man.

In psychology, the ego is our sense of autonomy, which is a somewhat false sense in that we are dependent on God for everything. We have borrowed our conscious awareness from God's conscious awareness. We have borrowed our body from the intelligent consciousness of material vibration. Our Soul, our pure essence, is an aspect of God. Even the idea of possessing "my time" and "my life" is part of the illusion of false autonomy. We are stewards of consciousness, body, time, Soul, and life.

When we try to take for ourselves what is not ours
(the fruits of our actions),
the consequence is a desperate need to control
and a paralyzing sense of responsibility

How freeing it would be if, for just one moment, we could feel to the depth of our being the utter simplicity of God's Will. What if it were as simple as:

Fulfill our allotted duties in life.
Serve our fellow man when we can.
And, keep our attention focused on God.

The great work of life is not to save the world but to attain God Realization which, by being in the process of doing so, you have a tremendously powerful and positive effect on the world condition and consciousness.

The great question of life
is not "what is it that I have come to do?"
but "who have I come to be?"

Purification

Purification is Silence removing the obstacles to ecstatic Union with God.

Purification is accomplished by putting God first. The first commandment in the Judeo-Christian tradition sums up the path of purification so simply: "Put God first—build your life around knowing, loving, and serving the Divine Beloved." Everything else is merely a commentary on this primary injunction.

As we pray and enjoin the Inner Self in Silence, our awareness of the presence of God within becomes stronger and stronger. This presence at once purifies and transforms us. Both are occurring simultaneously.

God's Presence is our purification

"The Living Flame, God Himself, invades us, but that which is supreme bliss is first experienced as purgation, for it destroys and consumes in us all that is alien to Him." [15]

73

Sometimes this is like taking a homeopathic remedy. Before the symptoms (suffering) are relieved, there is a healing crisis or a high fever that burns out what does not belong. Often those things (people, relationships, concepts, emotional patterns) that we try to fit in to, but that are alien to us and to the God within, are challenged and replaced by that which is more wholesome and supportive to one's reaching the Ultimate Goal. One saint humorously said that purification is very much like a cat coughing up a fur ball. It involves lots of noise and drama, but in the end, that which is not of the cat is gone and more room is left to take in better things.

Simply put – stuff comes up!

Anything and everything that keeps us from knowing and experiencing our Divine Nature will be "burning." Often people make the mistake of thinking that the "burning" or "going through things" is a sign that something is wrong. Or, they feel abandoned by God since they believe that the spiritual path is just one celestial delight after the other, so they question: What am I doing wrong? Where is God? If the spiritual path brings bliss, then why do I feel misery?

God is like the Divine Sculptor chipping away at the rough edges and pieces of stone that are foreign to our perfect reflection of Him. Does it hurt when He chips? Yes! But the sculptor is never closer to his work than when he is perfecting it. We cannot perfect ourselves. Our task is to be receptive to the "Word" doing Its work within us.

This purgation, this burning, is a sign of God's presence and activity within.

"God's presence within us is our purification,
Supreme Bliss is first experienced as purgation." [16]

Surrender

Surrender is Silence allowed.

It is letting go of what we have no control over. It is the first and last lesson on the spiritual path. There are three levels of surrender that we move through: the psychological or practical; the religious or spiritual; and the mystical. The first is the practical understanding of what we can control and what we cannot control. It is most succinctly phrased in the "Serenity Prayer:"

"God grant me the Serenity to accept the things

I cannot change,

the Courage to change the things I can,

and the Wisdom to know the difference." [17]

This first step alleviates much stress and begins the slow and steady process of letting go of control and experiencing inner peace and quietude.

This leads to a deeper religious, spiritual wisdom, which is the second understanding of surrender: "Everything that happens comes to us from God for a higher purpose. That purpose is to ultimately bring us Home to Him, and it can never be truly understood by the limited human mind." You have heard it said that everything happens for a reason. Everything happens for a very good reason! Even physicists tell us that the universe is intelligent and purposeful.

The last aspect of surrender is the mystical perspective, and that is: "God is the Sole Doer." This is His universe; we are acting our parts on a vast stage.

Fr. Jean Baptiste Saint-Lure wrote:

> *"Everything happens according to the Will of God. Have full faith in this...then every place, every moment, every event of your life begins to feel like heaven...and you become convinced that what is happening is meant for you."* [18]

Surrender draws Grace

Lord Jesus said: "Your Will, not mine, be done on earth as it is in heaven."[19]

When we give our life to God and serve God,

we surrender whatever little control we have

over what happens to us

.

When we get beyond the ego state of consciousness and per-spective, we realize that it is easy to let God be God instead of trying to act as God ourselves.

Truth is perceived differently

in different states of consciousness

At each state of consciousness perspective changes, paradigms shift. In ego consciousness, it is our very real experience that:

> There are many and we are separate from one another.

> We are the sole doers of our activity.

> Things can be equally perfect and imperfect.

From the state of Cosmic Consciousness, it is true that:

There is only one consciousness or God.

God is the sole doer.

All things are perfect.

And in the states between ignorance and full God Realization, there are many gradations and understandings of these truths.

In summary, the great act of surrender of the ego is summed up so beautifully and profoundly in this little verse:

"The Lord says:
If you give Me your mind,
I will give you My Heart."[20]

Faith

Faith is Silence knowing.

It is a deep intuitive knowing that everything is happening for a much bigger reason than we can possibly conceive of. And that purpose is fundamentally good, evolutionary, and will ultimately lead us to Mystical Union. It gives peace, draws grace, and allows us to receive the Spirit within. It is not exclusively associated with a belief system, and it is often transcendent to structured systems of beliefs.

Religions are sometimes called "faiths." Most "faiths" started with some great being having a profound experience of God and Ultimate Reality. Religion became the commentary of that experience. It developed into a set of prescriptions and proscriptions that ideally lead others to the same state of God Realization as the saint or seer around which the religion was formed.

Although the major religions of the world are tremendous repositories of wisdom, grace and comfort, sometimes they appear somewhat shallow on the surface. The deeper spiritual and mystical meanings of their scriptural messages are frequently lost on the very ones who are attempting to communicate them to us. Often these deeper truths are missed because the ones who teach are in a very, very different state of consciousness than the God-Realized Beings whose teachings they are trying to impart. It is like the painter who can see only in black and white. That painter can be a master of line and form and subtle shades of gray and shadow, but he fails miserably trying to describe to others the visual feast of a magnificent sunset. Many who flock to the churches and temples seeking the experience of God eventually feel a dryness and leave to experience something more.

So, too, the spirit in the meaning of the sacred words, the life-giving message, is often lost in their legalistic or literal meaning. **Those who cannot perceive the spirit of what is behind the sacred words cannot impart that deep spiritual meaning to others.** There is no fault here. It is the nature of duality that things come into being, flourish, and gradually die. But should the last Christian leave the face of the planet tomorrow, the veritable truths of the New Testament could be understood and experienced immediately by a Soul enjoined in the state of consciousness from which these words were written—one in communion with God. **In the state of Soul Consciousness and, more profoundly, in the various states of God Consciousness, the meaning and truths of sacred scripture become alive and become food for the heart.** One point of discrimination is very important to make: that is, pure religion "leads us back" to God. Religious organizations may be influenced by dogma, but don't confuse dogma with religion, or faith with an organization.

Dogma is like a thick layer of frozen ice
covering the ocean of Truth

Religion on the surface can be conflictual and confusing; however, **its essence cannot be easily dismissed.** At the root source of religion is the mystical experience of God. Saints are living proof of this.

These great saints did not disregard religion

They dove deeply into the source and
    essence of their own religions

They went beneath the surface and,
    using the bright light of their more highly evolved
    consciousness,

Saw God as He reveals Himself
    according to our consciousness—
    our capacity to receive

Faith is the opening to Ultimate Knowledge and Reality.

Faith is the mortal eyes seeing

the Divine Hand in the play of life

"To him who has faith, no explanation is necessary.

To him without faith, no explanation is possible."[21]

Knowing God

The mind (logic and reason) cannot investigate, experience, and know that which is beyond itself.

God reveals Himself through the heart (the core of one's being). God cannot be known by reading, theorizing, or thinking.

There are essentially three ways of knowing:

1. **Knowing via the Senses** (Empirical Knowledge): Through the experiences of the senses, knowledge is taken in and assimilated. Here one would attempt to experience God (the Essence) through His forms. What is experienced, in fact, is the "form" aspect of God but not the full nature of God. We see a partial reflection of God in His creation.

2. **Knowing via the Mind** (Logical Knowledge): Using reason and theory, we attempt to come up with a notion of a First Cause, a Supreme Being, an idea of God. However, the nature of God transcends any concepts the human mind can possible conceive of. Using the mind, we are as waves on the ocean attempting to understand the essence and true nature of the ocean by analyzing the surface patterns of the other waves. This only produces endless theories, purposes, meanings, and causalities which leads to a multiplicity of dogmatic religions.

3. **Knowing via Transcendent Intuition** (Mystical Experience): Through spiritual practices that purify the core (heart) of the human being and lead to the direct experience of God as the human being's natural state. Man is the capacity for God. Mystical "spiritual practices" purify the separate sense of self (ego) and bring the Soul into complete and permanent communion with God. Two primary means of ego purification are, (1) focusing the attention inwards on the inner states of God Realization, and, (2) practicing discrimination, which is the ability to continuously discern whether an action, thought, word or deed is, in fact, bringing us closer to our goal of Mystical Union, or leading us to distraction with the world of forms.

Do we choose the toys or the Toymaker?

True religion, the process of being lead back to God, is sustained not by teaching but by mystical experiences. Religion today often fails because it is perpetuated by unenlightened people who describe (incompletely) the "menu," without knowing the experience of the "meal." Over time, mainstream Christianity has degenerated from a LIVING REALITY to a set of social and moral principles.

Religious fundamentalism confuses letter for Truth.

Theology erroneously uses the human mind to try to understand that which transcends it!

Theological scholars expect to find the impossible—a historically accurate account of events of that time. They don't take into account that the events were written from many perspectives, from many different states of consciousness and their subsequent different understandings, and from different cultural references and different religious backgrounds over vast periods of time. Is it then surprising that they always find some level of seeming inaccuracy or contradiction? Modern forensic science has clearly demonstrated that two different people viewing the exact same situation will describe two very different sets of events. Now add time, different states of consciousness, different culture and languages, and we have the confusion and conflict about Living Truth that is rampant in Christianity and other religions today.

A person who imbibes the scriptural works partakes of the Divine Grace that inspired them! Spiritual texts embody the vibration of their authors. Reading texts such as the Bible, the Bhagavad-Gita, or the works of the great saints and Avatars who dwell in God Consciousness, activate the Living Truth within us and coax it into our conscious awareness. A partial list these great ones includes:

> Anandamayi Ma
> Annasuyi Devi
> Buddha
> Jesus
> John of the Cross
> Lawrence of the Resurrection
> Paramahansa Yogananda
> Ramakrishna
> Theresa of Avila

Many people who have just once read the great modern day spiritual classic *Autobiography Of A Yogi*[22], have testified to a profound change in their heart, the core of their being. And that is the point of scripture—scripture being the state of God Consciousness in word-form with the distinct ability to impart the quality of that state. We draw the essence or consciousness of that upon which we dwell.

Any concept of scripture when deeply contemplated and lived fully, can bring one to God Consciousness through its subtle spiritual vibration. Consider just one small aspect of the Christian scriptures such as: "Seek First the Kingdom and all else will come unto you."[23] Without the necessity of reading the Bible cover to cover, the pure understanding of this one teaching is enough to bring one to the full awareness of the Divinity within.

Each aspect of pure scripture is, in itself, a "portal" to Infinite Bliss Consciousness. If a castle has a thousand doors, it is only necessary to enter by one. However, the mind insists on exploring the history, fabric, builder, frame, and efficacy of as many doors as it can survey instead of simply "going through the door." The mind often takes great pride in being a perpetual "seeker," shunning the notion of being a "finder." (Karma?)

By focusing on a Truth, which is "wrapped up" in the word presentation of scripture, you attune to the Divine Energy that is the very Source of inspiration (Divine Consciousness) that led to the writing of the verses.[24]

The secrets of God cannot be unlocked by pure reason, but by the discrimination, sweetness, and nobility of a purified heart.

If all of the scriptures were lost,

they could be instantly rewritten,

because they are stored deep

in the hearts of saints

They are stored deep within

our most silent consciousness

The primary domain of True Religion is the direct experience of the "Ground of Being" or the Absolute Divine Principle, the Essence, which is the source and foundation of creation. What we have commonly practiced today is religion that addresses the "Field of Action"—the moral, social, intellectual aspects of creation's forms. It all comes down to "Essence" and "Form"…and what is the focus? True religion, as is life, is a mystery (beyond the mind) to be lived from the heart (core), and not a problem to be solved (by the fundamentalist or theological mind).

The essence of Christianity
is direct communion with God,
a realization of the reality of God within

Without that, we are stuck in a world
of inadequate intellectualism

One simple example serves to illustrate this richness of the depth of Christ's teaching and how some of it seems lost is in contemporary Christianity. Christ gave many messages, but there are three primary messages He gave to everyone. However, each person heard one more prominently than the others because that one was most appropriate and productive for that person's state of consciousness and growth at that time.

Christ's primary message to the masses was to love one another and keep the commandments.

To the more spiritually hungry, He told them that what they are looking for is the *"Kingdom of Heaven, which is within."* [25]

And to His nearest disciples He gave the mystical message of the Sermon on the Mount. More specifically, He encouraged them to strive for greater states of God Consciousness when He told them *"I and the Father are One."*[26] And that, in fact, the

Will of the Father is that we should become perfect (complete) as the Father in Heaven is Perfect. In other words, He said that God's Will is that we merge into the Supreme State of Ultimate Reality, the abode of the Unmanifest "Father," knowing ourselves as pure Spirit. Until then, and along the way, love one another, and seek the Peace, Joy, and Wisdom of the Inner Self, the Kingdom of Heaven within.

Patience

Patience is Silence confident.

Patience is the deep intuitive surety that comes from knowing that all things have their own time and all things come and go in cycles. Patience is the substance of serenity and the sister of faith and surrender. Patience frees us from the anxiety of change, the anxiety of excessive responsibility for results, and the anxiety that comes from the fear of lack of control. It is the spiritual fruit of "letting go and letting God." Like surrender and faith, patience does not imply passivity or lack of will. The patient ones are those who do everything necessary to attain the highest and most noble outcome conceivable, and at the end of the day give the outcome into God's Hands and let their efforts come to fruition according to Divine, not mortal, timing.

Sai Baba of Shirdi, the great Avatar of the early Twentieth Century, said that the most valuable virtues on the spiritual path are faith and patience.

Self-acceptance

Self-acceptance is Silence allowing itself to be in the process of becoming.

This is one of the most difficult of the healing virtues. The ego continually tells us that we are imperfect—not good enough. We compare ourselves to others and hold ourselves to standards that are impossible when in the ego state of consciousness. We try to love unconditionally, experience joy, have inner peace, and see life from a base of wisdom while being separated from the state of Love, Joy, Peace, and Wisdom—the state of the Soul, the State of Grace. We try to accomplish the impossible and hold ourselves to the inevitable sense of failure and inadequacy that goes with not attaining full results. How can we have these qualities without attaining the state from which they emanate? We have it backwards. Attain the state first and then the fruits of that state will be our constant experience.

Accepting ourselves just where we are, setting a goal, taking the necessary steps, and giving our selves **sufficient time** to achieve it is far more healthy, productive, and healing than making ourselves wrong and feeling inadequate. This feeling wrong and inadequate is a ploy of the ego to keep us bound and separate from our inner perfection.

Guilt is often a cover for anger, cowardice, and fear of moving forward.

The sense of personal inadequacy is almost always that lack of compassion and ignorance of the process of growth.

The greatest cause of the suffering, the cause of this painful non self-acceptance, is a keen sense of how we think things and others (including ourselves) "ought to be"—right now. We take a snapshot and miss the movie. Our perspective is limited to the immediate. We forget to remember that everything is in the process of becoming.

All of creation is eventually going to find its way Home

Love

Love is Silence flowing. It is the force of Wholeness that seeks Wholeness.

It is the force of Oneness (God) seeking the Unity of Its Parts. God's desire for us to reunite with Him is Love—that force that brings all of creation and all creatures back to their Source in Wholeness. Human love is a limited reflection of the Soul's need to be one with its Source.

God's Love is the force behind true spiritual evolution. This Love is purely and unconditionally expressed from the state of consciousness in which Love resides: the state of the Inner Self— Soul. It is the state of the Soul that draws us to oneness with God. In the ego state we settle for the counterfeit oneness with others and creation, which will never completely satisfy, thus we feel fundamentally lonely, inadequate, and separate from the Greater Whole.

Love is the force of Wholeness
that seeks Wholeness

Love is an evolutionary principle whose every expression brings all beings to a greater level of integrity and well-being. **It is the most evolutionary and most appropriate response to life. It is the spontaneous action of one immersed in the Peace, Joy, and Wisdom of the Soul.**

Love is the most evolutionary and most appropriate response to life

Pure Love is of the nature of God, the principle of the One, the force of completion, and the power of attraction that reunites the many with the One.

God is Love, in so far as God is calling us back to unity with Him, and is Himself that ecstatic state of completeness and power of attraction

The power of love is greater than the power of creation.
Creation is repulsion from Source. Love is drawing us out of creation and back to Source. Creation separates the many from the One. Spiritual evolution reunites the many with the One.

Love is the power of attraction

that reunites the many with the One

Love is a blending of heart and will, intellect and emotion. On the one hand, the **feminine aspect of love is the ecstasy of union**, on the other hand, the **masculine aspect of love is absolute commitment to duty and the highest good.**

Masculine love is expressed as devotion of body, heart, mind, and Soul to a noble ideal. It is the willingness to put the will of God and the needs of another, or the group, above our individual needs. There are many examples of this in everyday life, from the daily sacrifices of mothers and fathers for their children and each other, to the extraordinary acts of love evidenced by the heroism of policeman, firefighters, and soldiers, to cosmic events such as Christ giving Himself on the cross for the welfare of humanity. His Holy Life, this supreme act of love, was also a supreme event in man's spiritual evolution.

Jesus once said: *"He who seeks to save his life shall lose it, and he who loses his life shall find it."*[27]

All forms of love are a reflection

of the Soul's yearning

to become united again with its Divine Beloved

In its more feminine manifestation (and here masculine and feminine refer to principle, not gender!), love is the desire to merge with the object of attraction and the ecstasy of completion (devotion).

On the universal level, love is the complete appreciation of the "essence" of the object of devotion.

Love's masculine nature is duty.

Love's feminine nature is merging.

Love's universal nature is pure appreciation.

Often "romantic love" is mistaken for "spiritual communion." But this human love is the attempt for completion with another part, another incompleteness, and not completion with the Whole—or God. Seeking completion in human love invariably leads to disappointment. This disappointment can lead to the never ending search for the perfect "soul mate," or it can lead to deeper spiritual seeking. The Soul's only mate is God. The rest is the illusion of the ego.

The Soul's only "soul mate" is God

Human love is pure and unconditional only to the degree that the individual has reached the self-sufficiency of the Soul. Until then, human ego needs to keep the full, unconditional expression of love somewhat limited.

Love can never be reduced to a set of behaviors or attitudes that suppress feelings that are natural when in ego states of consciousness. We cannot "learn" to love unconditionally. Love is the fruit of a state of consciousness. It is the natural state of being absorbed in the nature of the Soul—Inner Self.

Ego and mind imply separation. Love is unity.

Learning implies that there is a lesson that the mind can comprehend, master, and use to control emotions and attitudes. It implies sets of standards for behavior, yet we see from the lives of the Great Ones that **love transcends any fixed descriptors. We cannot learn unconditional love. To love unconditionally, we must become Love. And love is the natural outcome of union with the Inner Self or Soul.**

Love is life flowing from a state of consciousness
from which stems all the thoughts,
deeds, and actions that are most appropriate
to the evolution of the other

The great master of Love, Jesus Himself, went into the temple with whips and beat the money changers and sent them on their way. To the limited mind that does not square with today's standards of loving behaviors, and that event seems to be quite "unloving." But we mistake kindness for love. Kindness is a quality of action. **Love is the principle of action. It is not a quality of behavior!** Love is not necessarily kindness. Kindness is kindness. Love is that which causes evolutionary growth, bringing us ultimately to God.

Love is the principle of action
It is not a quality of behavior

When we relegate such a profound

principle as Love

to a set of learned behaviors and attitudes,

the magnitude of its depths

and magnificence of its divinity becomes trivialized

On the surface of things, masculine love can seem unloving until we remember that loving is also an evolutionary principle. For example, a loved one locking a destructive, addicted alcoholic family member out of his home and forcing him to stay away until he recognizes that he has a problem and gets needed help can be performing a loving, life saving act. That's an example of masculine love, and it is every bit as "loving" in its nature as the mother who misses a meal so that her baby can eat.

To often we mistake the expression of love
for the nature of Love!

Remember, too, that Jesus fiercely represented His principles. Sometimes He expressed this love in great kindness, and at other times He expressed His love with force, such as when he called the scribes and Pharisees "hypocrites" and "brood of vipers" and swept the temple clean of the money changers who desecrated its spirit. Love cannot be judged by outer appearances.

"Seek first the Kingdom of Heaven within." [28]
That is where Love is
and from that state you become Love
and Love's perfect instrument of expression

Jesus gave the great commandment: *"Love God with your whole heart, mind, soul, and strength; and love your neighbor as yourself."* [29] This is a magnificent example of all three aspects of Love.

"Love God" reflects the feminine aspect of merging with the object of devotion.

"Love your neighbor" reflects the masculine aspect of putting the highest good of the other at least as high on your priorities as your own highest good.

And **"Love yourself"** reflects the universal principle of appreciating the essence of something—yourself, the Soul, which is a perfect aspect of God within.

To truly love
is to adopt the state of Inner Silence
and act from there

Grace

Grace is Silence in activity. It is the outcome of knitting the values of both silence and activity within one's being. It is the fruit of the balance between the inner and the outer values of life.

It is the full value of the Inner Life flowing through us without impediment. It is the continuous expression of the qualities of the Soul, which are Joy, Love, Wisdom, and Inner Peace. It is the equanimity of spirit that allows; it is an experience of life in harmony with ourselves and our Source.

Grace allows and is an expression of peace of mind. This peace of mind is an integral aspect of the spiritual path that leads to God Union. The mind must be relaxed to receive and recognize the presence of God within. Tension and control conceal our true nature.

Grace is attained through surrender, faith, patience, and self-acceptance. It is the fruit of realizing deeply the three Truths:

> **Everything that is happening is happening according to a greater plan that is ultimately in our best interest.**
>
> **There is a Loving Being watching over every detail of our lives.**
>
> **How it ought to be is exactly as it is inevitably unfolding.**[30]

Through self-effort, we can draw grace to us through the attitudes of surrender, faith, patience, and self-acceptance.

Grace is the ability to handle whatever God gives us in this life.

It is the gift to those who give their hearts and lives to God.

When God gives us Grace

He gives us a taste of His Infinite Inner Peace

Anxiety, a sense of separateness, and an eerie inner fear that somehow we are inadequate and not good enough, are the offspring of an over-exaggerated sense of responsibility, the need to be in control, and the desire to hold on staunchly to how we think "it ought to be." This is especially predominant today since we are lead to believe that we can have whatever we want if we visualize, believe, and try hard enough. This belief is the ego usurping the creative powers of God as its very own! It is a complete misunderstanding of the role of corrective karma and the need for the mind to be pure and in a high state of Unity Consciousness before it can manifest reality at will. Great God-Realized Beings can manifest and create at will because they have control of the laws of nature and are in perfect attunement with God's Will for the Divine Plan. Our personal reality is created by karma and consciousness, not by mental beliefs. Our personal reality is the perspective of our consciousness and identity and our ensuing understanding is paraphrased in the shorthand of "beliefs." Consciousness is the cause; beliefs are the effects.

At the root of causality is our identity and state of consciousness which dictates our philosophy and perspective. Our philosophy and perspective dictates our beliefs and attitudes, which further govern our emotions and experience of reality. To change the experience of reality it is necessary to go the source of our structure, our consciousness. When that changes, everything that falls from it (i.e., perspective, beliefs and experience), change also.

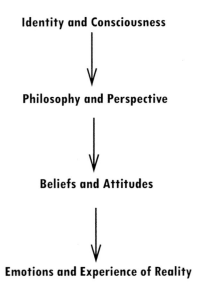

Identity and Consciousness

Philosophy and Perspective

Beliefs and Attitudes

Emotions and Experience of Reality

So, the "belief" that if you change your beliefs, your fundamental reality will change is another partial truth that looks good on the surface but lacks the necessary depth of understanding. To change our experience of reality, of which beliefs are only a part, is a much bigger task that involves our state of consciousness. In changing our state of consciousness, our beliefs and the experience of reality change naturally. The discussion of whether beliefs cause an experience or an experience causes a belief is an irrelevant attempt of the mind to understand the process of change that has at its very essence identity and consciousness.

In summary, Grace transcends law. In the State of Grace, equanimity and peace of mind are untouched by the crashing waves of karma. Law demands certain karmic events in our lives as well as the overshadowing experience that accompanies them. Grace does not prevent the law from being fulfilled, but it gives us the ability to experience karma with equanimity. Grace detaches us firmly and finally from the jaws of duality.

In the State of Grace
equanimity and peace of mind are untouched
by the crashing waves of karma

God's Will

Generally, God's Will is "What Is"

Specifically, God's Will is for us to find Him and realize our oneness with Him. "Be perfect as the Father in heaven is Perfect;" that is, to know yourself as pure spirit.

God's Will is also that we get ourselves lost in the process by forgetting who we are. It is both directional and specific. That means that God's Will can contain all apparent opposites. It can appear that there is "God's Will" and a separate will called "man's will," and that they can be in opposition to one another. In dualistic reality that may seem true. But in Truth, it is impossible!

God's Will for us is clearly that (in time) we realize Him. It is also that we use our own will to make this choice. Now, in the process of using our own will, we can and will get lost but that, too, is part of the grand plan. We have the freedom to get lost. And God has set up the elaborate laws of karma to give us feedback as well as gifts of grace to ease our way home. Note the parallel to the parable of the prodigal son, who was given the freedom to leave his father's house, squander his fortune, and then come home to a grand celebration.

So, in essence, when we are in the state of thick, heavy ego consciousness doing, thinking, and being all those things that take us farther away from God...well, that's part of it all. It would appear that we are in opposition to God's Will from a limited perspective, but from the bigger picture the entire play of creating this universe and concealing and revealing Himself is part of God's own desire. His desire is to experience Himself within His own creation with its limitation and duality.

God's Will for us is not so much what we choose, but that we can choose. His Will for us is that we eventually choose Him, but it is also His Will that we choose whatever we want. Until we choose Him, however, we get the fruits of our choices for other things. God's Will contains all pairs of opposites.

The free and open space in between

our inevitable karma

is where free will comes in

Our will is free to the degree that we are not predisposed by our karma to think, act, and experience in a certain way. Karma is either neutralized by experiencing the fruits of our past actions, or is burned in the fires of spiritual practice. Although karma must be endured, when experienced from the State of Silence (Soul), karma is virtually irrelevant; it cannot affect the inner states of Love, Peace, Wisdom, and Joy.

Nothing can overshadow the State of Grace—

the inner states of

Peace, Love, Joy, and Wisdom

So there are three perspectives from which to view the truth of God's Will:

The first is that God's Will is specific:

Do your duty and fulfill your responsibilities.

Serve your neighbor.

Attain Self Realization.

The second view is that God's Will is all inclusive, containing His Will that we choose. And some of those choices can appear to be in opposition of His Will for us —moving us away from Him.

The ultimate view, or the mystical view, is that God's Will is absolute and that, in effect, God is the Sole Doer.

Wisdom

Wisdom is seeing the finite through the eyes of the infinite. It is to see and act from higher perspectives. It is the value of Silence within perception and thought.

It is knowing that the limited mind can never fully know the Unlimited God. The limited mind can get a glimpse through science of God's incredible power and intelligence, but the mind cannot feel the Divine Heart and its Infinite Love. Wisdom gives us the awareness that the function of the mind is to describe the pieces of the many and the function of the heart is to reunite those pieces into the One.

As the mind looks out into duality

the heart pulls us back to our One Source

Ego dwells in the mind

God dwells in the heart

Wisdom, like Love, Peace, and Joy, dwells naturally in the state of Silence, or Soul Consciousness and whatever perspective is taken while immersed in that state will be of Wisdom.

Wisdom cannot be attained

but the state from which Wisdom

emanates can be attained

and from that state Wisdom

(like Love, Peace, and Joy)

is our natural life perspective

There are numerous stories of illiterate and unschooled saints who could expound on the most complex meanings of sacred scripture. That is because their state of consciousness was the same state from which the scripture was communicated. Wisdom in the Soul state is the first stage of omniscience, which is one of the primary aspects of the state of God Consciousness.

Knowledge is of the ego state

Wisdom is of the Soul state

Omniscience is of the God-Realized state

The Lord says:

"If you give me your mind,

I will give you My heart." [31]

Virtue

Virtue is the expression of Silence in our character.

Virtues are the fruits of watering the root of our being—the tree of life. Virtues flow naturally when our center of being is fixed in the Inner Self. All virtues are variations or modulations of Silence. They are personal expressions of Love, Wisdom, Peace, and Joy.

All virtues spring from the state of the Inner Self.

Someone once wrote:

> **"What does the love of God do to a person?**
>
> > **It kills his desires**
> > **It purifies his heart**
> > **It protects him**
> > **It banishes vices**
> > **It incurs rewards**
> > **It lengthens life**
> > **It cleanses the Soul."**

The great ones tell us that the most effective way to develop virtues and discard vice is to immerse one's self in the state of Soul. This is the state from which all virtue flows and from which all vices are extinguished. This state of Peace, Love, Joy, and Wisdom imprints the conscious mind with stronger and more evolutionary thought forms and patterns of living than those that are not supportive to our overall well-being and spiritual evolution.

Often focusing on a fault keeps it empowered. It is far more productive to strive to change consciousness rather than to struggle exclusively with thought, belief, emotion, or behavior. Focusing on our weakness and not focusing on our strengths leads to very strong weaknesses and very weak strengths. Virtues are the manifestation of the fruits of our spirit.

Truth

Truth is the nature of God, which is Unchanging—Consciousness, Existence, and Bliss.

When Jesus said, *"I shall give you truth and the truth will set you free,"* [32] He promised the possibility of Truth (God)—God Consciousness that releases us from the bounds, karmas, and suffering of duality. Truth is not dogma. "Truth" is more than the simple consistent arrangement of facts. It is the Essence of God. It is the Essence of His Nature. Truth is "I AM." However, when this "I AM" identifies with an object of perception, such as "I am a man," or "I am a woman," It forgets Its true nature and takes on limitation—or ego. These objects of perception are relative, or subject to change. The "I AM" (God) is Changeless and beyond relativity.

Joy

Joy is Silence cherished.

It is the effervescent contentment with what is.

We know Joy when we are happy to take from life what is given. When we experience the Joy of the Soul and higher states of consciousness, this Joy is the essence of completion and fulfillment. There is nothing that can add to it or take away from it. It is our natural state. (And yet the delusion is to try to find Joy outside in the world of changes.)

True Joy is expressed by the happiness
of taking from life what is given

Suffering comes from trying to take
from Life what is not given

Silence

Silence vibrating is Creation
Silence flowing is Love
Silence shared is Friendship

Silence seen is Infinity
Silence heard is the Name of God
Silence expressed is Beauty

Silence maintained is Strength
Silence omitted is Suffering
Silence experienced is Peace

Silence recorded is Sacred Scripture
Silence preserved is the Mystical Path
Silence given is Grace

Silence received is Joy
Silence perceived is Wisdom
Silence stabilized is Realization

Silence alone Is [33]

The Three Types of Spiritual Paths

Wisdom

Devotion

Service

The spiritual path that is most compatible with our temperament is the path that is right for us. The path we choose must fulfill our nature. These three paths parallel the primary elements of life's highest purpose, which are to know, love, serve, and merge with God. They also represent the paths of mind, heart, and body. The goal of each path is to reverse the life current and achieve freedom from the ego and its bonds of attachments, misunderstandings, and self-centeredness.

According to the words of a Sanskrit hymn:

> *As the different streams*
> *Having sources in different places*
> *All mingle their water in the sea, so, O Lord,*
> *The different paths which people take,*
> *Through various tendencies,*
> *Various though they appear*
> *Crooked or straight,*
> *All eventually lead to Thee.*

Usually, we are not exclusively on one path. The paths intersect and weave through one another. It is only because of our unique temperaments and approaches that the paths seem different. They each use similar methods of spiritual practice, and each have the same goal of God Union whether the concept of God is an idea of God without form or God with form. Although ultimately God is formless, it is often useful to have a loving, attractive idea of God in form as we progress along our journey.

The Path of Wisdom

This is the path of knowing who we truly are. It is knowing the Ultimate Truth that there is but One Consciousness, One Doer, and it is All Perfect. The path of Wisdom is one of self-inquiry.

Using the spiritual practices of meditation, chanting, prayer, practicing the presence, and self-inquiry, the aspirant gradually expands his consciousness and identity to express and experience "Truth" more fully in philosophy, perspective, attitude, beliefs, actions, emotions, and general experiences of life.

The ultimate goal of the Path of Wisdom is *"I and My Father Are One"* [34]—Cosmic Consciousness, knowing one's self as pure Spirit.

"Be perfect as the Father in Heaven is perfect." [35]

Cosmic Consciousness is the fruit of meditation, the redirection of the life energy in and up instead of down and out. It is the state of seeing the finite from the eyes of the Infinite. It involves quieting the mind and merging into higher states of consciousness.

The Path of Devotion

This is the path of relationship, the path of the heart, the path of Love. Devotion is a commitment as well as an expression of sublime fullness.

Devotion is said to be the easiest path since it is the natural inclination of each individual to be attracted back to its source. A deep and abiding love for God and/or one of His many aspects as guru, teacher, saint, or Divine Manifestation (Avatar) characterizes this path.

"Love is a fire in the heart
that burns up all but the Beloved's wishes." [36]

This devotional love can have the feminine aspect dominant wherein there is an ecstatic feeling of union, or the masculine aspect where there is great satisfaction in the fulfillment of duty to one's favored form of a personal God. On this path the aspirant may use the same spiritual tools as on the path of wisdom and reach the same states and ultimate goals. However, the approach is that of "relationship." He, the devotee, joyously makes God responsible for all events of his life and in full surrender never takes his mind away from his Divine Beloved. His personal desires are transformed into the one compelling desire to please God.

The desire to please God
is the fulfillment of all desires

The Path of Selfless Service

Pure selfless service extinguishes the ego so that only God remains.

Selfless service is selfless because the devotee gives up completely the fruits of his action and the notion of ownership. This is the path of renunciation. It is giving up the sense of ownership of body, comforts, self (ego) satisfaction, and even our own sense of possessing our own "time" in order to be in the service of God and Love.

Selfless Service is living life as an act of love

As the wax of a candle burns itself joyfully in service to the flame, on this path we give our lives to God and let Him do with us as He pleases. This surrender is the core of the path of selfless service.

"I and the Father are One." [37]

— Path of Wisdom

"Love God with your whole heart, mind, body, Soul and strength." [38]

— Path of Devotion

"Love your neighbor." [39]

— Path of Service

How do we love God? We love God by doing His Will. Sometimes it is joyful and sometimes it is a struggle. It is always making the highest good our first priority. And that highest good is to fulfill our responsibilities, serve our neighbors, and to attain God Realization.

Love is not an emotion

It is an evolutionary force

It is a profound commitment

to an ideal of Wholeness

that fulfills our Inner Longing

Spiritual Practice

Spiritual practice is the process of refocusing the mind and drawing it toward its Source.

The nature of mind is like water. Water does not have form, but it will take the form of the container we pour it into. Spiritual practices are a pouring of the mind into the forms of consciousness that are greater than itself. It is drawing to itself the essence of that which we put our attention on. It is the contemplation of God—with or without form. It is as alive and as useful for a Buddhist and Hindu as it is for a Christian, Muslim, or Jew.

There are six primary practices on the path of Mystical Spirituality. These are by no means mutually exclusive, and most people's personal practices involve some of each:

Meditation
Chanting
Selfless Service
Prayer and Practicing the Presence
Self-inquiry
Scriptural Reading

Meditation

Meditation is merging with Silence.[40] It is the act of being aware of our true nature by turning the attention within and drawing the energy in and up to the higher centers of consciousness. The focus of meditation is Divine Communion.

The Name of God or Mantra
is the sound of Silence

This receptivity to experiencing our Divine Nature can most easily be developed by giving the mind a Name of God (mantra) upon which to dwell.

The name of God constitutes the sound form or seed essence of God who then enters the boundaries of the finite mind and heart and begins to work a process of expansion that leads to the full manifestation of God Consciousness.

Using the Name of God is the same as merging with Him, becoming united with Him, and experiencing His Nature as Consciousness, Existence, and Bliss; or, in the early stages, Peace, Joy, Love, and Wisdom.

123

Pure mystical meditation is focus and communion with God without the expectation of gifts. Sitting and waiting for experiences is sitting and waiting for experiences. It is not meditation. It is expectation. Mystical meditation is an opportunity to practice Love. **God will come when He will come. Our task is to be receptive to the work of the "Word" or presence of God within us.**

Sometimes it may seem as if nothing is happening in meditation. However, from a larger perspective, that is not so. Each time we use the Name of God, it is like a drop of water dripping into an inkwell whose walls are crusted with dried ink. With each drop of water (or repetition of the Name of God) a little bit of the ink is removed until the glass becomes transparent and pure.

Purification is God's Presence within us just as much as an ecstatic or peaceful or joyous experience is God's Presence within us. Of course, we prefer the one to the other, but they are in many ways the same. Again, don't mistake the form for the essence.

True meditation is not yearning for visions, paranormal phenomena, or thrilling experiences. The path to the Divine is not a circus! It is emptying the self so that the Presence of God may overtake us.

What you think upon, you attract
What the mind dwells upon, you become

Chanting

Chanting is manifesting consciousness through sacred sounds—the Name of God. Sound is the source and the mother of all creation. Sound creates the potential for certain states of consciousness to manifest. Since the mind takes on any shape upon which it focuses, and consciousness has the ability to assume any shape at will, expressing (chanting) sacred sounds brings our consciousness to the states of higher consciousness that these sounds represent.

Chanting purifies the desires
that bind us to the ego

Chanting is a very effective way to start meditation. It clears the conscious mind and relaxes the emotional state. It prepares us to dive deep within to access higher states. Chanting, like meditation, uses the thought or sound of a Sacred Name of God. It is like superimposing the blueprints or patterns of silence and peace over the personal blueprint or patterns of personal karmas and excitation. It breaks up unhealthy or negative thought and energy patterns in our consciousness.

The sound of a sacred chant changes and raises the "vibrations" of all that it permeates. Some say that chanting is a highly effective means of passive meditation, since the chant meditates us, we don't meditate the chant.

The sacred sounds of chanting
actually meditate us

They purify and uplift us and everyone and everything in our environment.

Selfless Serving

Selfless Serving is making our life an act of Love.

It is an active life of personal "unselfing" that diminishes the firm grip of the ego by putting aside our personal desires and working to tend to the needs of others. (Note here the use of the words *desires* and *needs!*) It is offering all of ourselves—our thoughts, words, deeds, and the actions of our body, mind, and spirit—in the service of God, the evolutionary aspect of God's Nature, which is Love. This is accomplished in many ways such as alleviating the suffering of the body in sickness, the mind in ignorance, or the heart in loneliness; or by deep prayer for the welfare of humanity through prayer in Silence.

The path of Selfless Service asks that we do our best and leave the fruits of our action to God. We give God ourselves, our actions, and the fruits of our action. It is truly renunciation in activity. It is an expression of "Silence in activity."

"I saw my Lord in a dream and I asked,

'How am I to find You?'

He replied, 'Leave your self and come.'" [41]

Sometimes the path of service is misconstrued as a life of social action whose end point is a perfect world. The end point of Mystical Spirituality will always remain the realization of our Union with God. Selfless service eliminates the negative ego, thus allowing God to take full possession of us. Selfless service is a valuable spiritual practice.

"For what does it profit a man
to gain (or save) the world,
and lose his Soul?"[42]

Prayer and Practicing the Presence

Prayer is a transformational process. It is the consent to God's Presence within us, the receptivity to God working within us.

Prayer works at the deepest levels of the human heart (the core of one's being) and leads to true spiritual progress and healing. Those who practice continuous prayer experience their nature as transcendent and leave behind all remnants of the lower self. Prayer works mystically, beyond the mind, and serves to bring the individual to the experience of Divine Love.

At the very instant that the human being feels the power of God's Infinite Love, every other worldly sensation becomes inconsequential in contrast.

The perfect prayer as described by St. John of the Cross is to **stand unprotected before God who will then take possession of us (once again!).** Our prime duty on the spiritual path is to nurture our inner spiritual receptivity. Mystical prayer is very similar to meditation. The object is God and the destination is God's Presence.

As meditation is allowing awareness

of our true nature,

Prayer is the consent to God's Presence within us

This is not the same as the popular notion of "being in the present." Practicing the Presence of God is the fruit of what is called the contemplative life, wherein no matter how strenuous the mental activity, the awareness of God is always foremost in our being. It is being in the present with God. It is being present with the nature of Love, Wisdom, Peace, and Joy. It is not being "in the present" with the heightened awareness of the ego's sense of itself and the external environment as the primary object of awareness. "Practicing the Presence" is of eternity; "being in the present" is being fully aware of the finite.

Practicing the Presence is the natural state of Love, Peace, Wisdom, and Joy that is easily accessed when keeping the Name of God on the lips or in the heart during activity. It is the product of what is called by St. Paul "continuous prayer" or "prayer without ceasing."

Practicing the Presence is experiencing
the blissful states of the Inner Self

In the Vedic tradition, constantly repeating the Name of God internally is called "japa yoga" and is a form of Practicing the Presence. In the West, the Jesus Prayer, or centering prayer, is used as effectively and many, many saints have achieved their states through the instrumentation of the Jesus Prayer.[43]

A great Avatar of our time, Anandamayi Ma, said:

> *"Choose a word, a form, an image, a symbol—in fact anything sacred representing Him as a whole or in part—and, whether in happiness or in misery, ceaselessly direct the current of your*

thinking towards it. Even though the mind may repeatedly wander here and there, it will again seek rest in this center. In due course love and devotion will awaken for Him who will then take possession of your heart.

"Although God is ever present within as well as without, it is necessary to keep His remembrance awake in all one's thoughts and actions. For the tendencies acquired in countless former births bind man with such force that the quest for God does not come to him easily."[44]

May God empty my very self of all except His own Presence

"The perfect mystic is not an ecstatic devotee lost in contemplation of an abstract Oneness, not a saintly recluse shunning all comment with mankind, but the "true saint" goes in and out amongst the people and eats and sleeps with them and buys and sells in the market and marries and takes part in social intercourse; and never forgets God for a single moment."[45]

Self Inquiry

This is a relentless practice of asking under all circumstances and at all times: "Who am I?"

And coming to the identification point of the Formless God.

In practicing the process of self inquiry over periods of time, there begins the phenomenon in which the individual awareness begins to disengage itself from the ego identification and begins to witness the "I" of the "I am that (object)." This process, when followed to its conclusion, can lead one to Supreme Realization of Union with the Formless Absolute God.

Some try to use this technique without guidance. However, few are ever successful without a teacher. The great saint Ramana Maharshi is one of the foremost exponents of this path during modern times and at one time stated that self inquiry could lead to the ultimate reality without a teacher. At the end of his life, though, he did say that it is necessary to have a Guru-Teacher to lead you along the way. It is much too difficult to reach the final destination without a God-Realized guide.

Scriptural Reading

Scripture is consciousness in the form of thought communicated through word symbols.

Words are used to describe the Unbounded Presence and Truth within bounded and limited reality. Reading sacred scripture eliminates misconception and "rewires" the human mind to receive Truth.

As the outer form of the scriptures seems to be moralistic, the inner meaning of scripture is unlimited consciousness expressed in limited form. These forms are not Truth in themselves, but they point to Truth. They are not the star in the heavens but the signs that point the way.

Reading scripture from the state of Silence allows us to go to the source consciousness from which the scriptures were written. It follows that an unenlightened teacher is apt to teach a completely different meaning of sacred texts than a saint or an Avatar such as Jesus.

Our personal state of consciousness dictates

the level and the amount of scripture

that we can understand

The inner meaning of the scriptures is what works changes in people's hearts. Our understanding of them is like a personal measure of our spiritual attainment. To look only at the meaning of the words is to obfuscate the true meaning of the essence that they are meant to convey. Here again, we can mistake form for essence.

We read scripture to superimpose Truth
on the incomplete understanding
found in relative knowledge

The stories and writing of saints are impregnated with their consciousness and can lead us to clearer understanding and states of inner peace and bliss. Contemplating scripture activates the invisible structure of Truth and Truth's expressed energy patterns lying dormant within our consciousness.

Definitions of Spiritual Practice

Meditation is merging with Silence.

Chanting is manifesting consciousness through sacred sounds—the Names of God.

Selfless Serving is making life an act of Love.

Prayer is the consent to God's Presence within us.

Practicing The Presence is maintaining the Silence while in activity.

Self-Inquiry is using pure awareness to discover the "I AM."

Scriptural Reading is consciousness in the form of thought communicated through word symbols. It superimposes Truth on knowledge found in the relative. It activates the energy and forms of Truth within us. [Scriptural reading is explained in detail in the book *Heart of the Mystic*, also by Jerry Thomas.]

Nothing short of the direct experience of God
will ever satisfy our needs for
wholeness, fulfillment, and completion

One and Three – The Trinity

Mathematics, metaphysics, and mysticism seem to be based on the expression of the One in Three, or in triplicities. God as the Trinity entails:

> The Absolute Unmanifest beyond creation aspect of **Father,**

> The sole reflection of the Father's Consciousness within Creation, which is the **Son,**

> And the intelligence matrix of Creation Itself, which is the **Holy Spirit**, also known as the Divine Mother, the Creator aspect of God, the sound of "Om" and Amen, and in ancient Christianity, the Virgin Mary.

The Trinity is expressed and experienced in the three states of what mystics call God Consciousness:

> Consciousness of God (**Father**) beyond Creation is **Cosmic Consciousness.**

> Consciousness of God (**Son**) within Creation is **Unity or Christ Consciousness.**

> And consciousness of God (**Mother**) as Creator is **God Consciousness.**

Imagine for a moment a vast expanse of space filled with an all-pervading blue light (Pure Essence—the Father).

Now imagine a vast crystal ball that represents the matrix, form, and substance of all form (the manifest consciousness of the Mother, Creator God, the Holy Spirit, the sound of the eternal OM).

Now see the reflection of the Father (the blue light) permeating the crystalline matrix of Creation (Mother). That is the sole reflection of God the Father within creation (this is the Son).

The individualized aspect of God within creation is the Soul. Each Soul has a covering that hides its true nature, called the ego, that sense of separation that believes itself to be the sole doer and sees itself as imperfect. As we reverse the downward flow of the creation process and attain Mystical Union, our perspective is quite different. We see:

There is only One Consciousness
There is only One Doer
Everything is Perfect

The Spiritual Process

Along with the Cosmic dreamer, we dream a separate exist-ence. The spiritual process is about waking from this Cosmic Dream. It is about:

Moving from excitation to Silence.
Having Silence as the inner experience.
Uniting successively with the three aspects of Divinity

God as Creator
God within Creation
God beyond Creation

The spiritual process is about
waking from the dream of Creation
and going beyond duality

The Teacher

The True Teacher does not give knowledge alone. The True Teacher gives us Ultimate Reality. The True Teacher is the one who can carry us over the worldly delusion to reach this Eternal Goal.

Many paths take us to many places, many realities, and there are many guides along the way. However, on the path to Mystical Union, only one who is in Mystical Union can show the way. Many can describe the menu, but only the host can provide the feast.

From the *Bhagavad Gita*:

> **Whenever there is a decay of righteousness and an ascendancy of unrighteousness, I manifest Myself: and for the protection of the virtuous, the destruction of the vicious and for the establishment of righteousness, I manifest Myself in age after age.**

In ages past we have had such avatars (manifestations of the full Consciousness in a human form) as Krishna, Jesus, and Buddha. They demonstrated their Cosmic Consciousness by virtue of their mastery of the three aspects of the Divine: Omniscience, Omnipotence, and Omnipresence. They healed the sick, raised the dead, and changed the course of the forces of nature. Anything and anyone with whom they contacted was affected by the power of their Love—the evolutionary force that brings us to God.

In our own age, God has showered us with numerous modern-day manifestations of His Very Self (Avatars) in male and female form. They include the deathless Babaji, Paramahansa Yogananda, Ramakrishna, Shirdi Sai Baba, Anandamayi Ma, Annasuya Devi, and beloved Ammachi—who is still in human form and can be readily approached.

Mystical knowledge is so subtle that it can be known only from the state of consciousness in which it resides. The mind can't possibly bring us to states that it cannot grasp. We need a divine guide.

Amma Mata Amritanandamayi Ma, "Ammachi," says:

> *"Human effort is not sufficient enough to remove the deep-seated human tendencies. God's Grace and the Teacher's Grace is a must. It is only then that the mind can be taken to the Ultimate Subtle State where there are no thoughts and no mind—only Being."* [47]

As art reveals beauty,
the God-Realized Teacher reveals God

To know God, one needs a God-Realized Being to give guidance, remove karma, and help the suffering human to focus on his true nature—the God within. Although through the teachings we will be in attunement with Truth, we need guidance, help, and protection to prevent us from getting sidetracked from the goal. The Cosmic Dream (illusion) is so subtle that it can easily make our minds veer off in the wrong direction without our recognizing it.

So the three attributes of the True Mystical Teacher (Guru) are that the Guru can:

Remove our karma

Guide us in Truth

Give us the experience of God [48]

We can go only as far as those whom we choose to teach us! Aim for the highest consciousness, the highest teachers—God in form!

The One Great Spiritual Commandment

Know God first...the rest is merely commentary.

The Grand Spiritual Technique

Keep your focus on God.

God's Will

Do your allotted duty. Take care of your responsibilities. Your karma brought them to you.

Whenever you can, serve others.

"Be Perfect..." [49] Attain Mystical Union. Know yourself as pure Spirit.

The Mystical Life

God is simple; everything else is complex.

The life of a mystic is simplicity itself. To a mystic, this life is not centered on a grandiose sense of needing to "do" something external. It focuses not on what we do, but who we become. It is measured not in outer accomplishment, but by the depth of our Self Realization. Its effects on the human race and material nature are profound. This life concerns itself with changing consciousness, not beliefs and conditions. Conditions are the products of consciousness. When you change the root cause of conditions (consciousness), then right conditions emerge spontaneously.

The Mystical Path is about living life outside the boundaries or dream of duality. It does not concern itself so much with creating a personal reality as much as realizing Ultimate Reality. The purpose of the mystical path is that we express our true nature, which is a merging of individual self into the Source of Self Itself—Divine Union.

This is not a path of the Old Age, nor is it the path of the New Age. It is ageless, as is its message:

Nothing short of the direct experience of God
will ever satisfy our need for
wholeness, fulfillment, and completion

143

Beyond the ego's personal reality, the Mystical Path fulfills the Soul's destiny to know and become one with Ultimate Reality. It assumes with great confidence that the human being returning to God is the pinnacle of creation. The Mystical Life is an Act of Love.

It is not about taking possession of God, but allowing God to take possession of us.

It is about receptivity, not struggle. God is seeking us.

It is not focused on what we get, but what we give.

It is a path of allowing, not expecting.

It is not about achieving a goal so much as fulfilling our potential.

It is an emptying of the self and becoming full with God.

It is allowing God to live His Life through us.

It is complete surrender to the Will of God and absolute service to His Command through the Christ, *"Be Ye Perfect as the Father in Heaven is Perfect"*[50] (know your true identity as Spirit —attain the highest state of unity with God by becoming One with Him and complete therefore in Him), and "Love God with your whole mind, heart, body and strength; and then, love your neighbor as you love yourself." [51]

It is expending the individual life in service to Divine Life as the wax of a candle gives itself in service to the flame.

The Mystical Life is a complete and selfless Act of Love to the Divine Beloved.

Changing impermanent conditions won't change consciousness. However, when consciousness changes, conditions permanently change.

The Mystical Life starts with dissatisfaction with life's status quo. It is fueled by the desire to have suffering stop and Joy, which is our true nature, begin. Along the way we find teachers who promise much but disappoint even more. We often become convinced that we can do it ourselves, only to find that:

Personal autonomy is too high a price

to pay for loss of Divine Union

We rebel against Surrender, mistake Faith for weakness, and disregard Wisdom and Patience for immediate results, results, results!

We look to self-empowerment
only to find that we are empowering the wrong self!

As the ego gets stronger, our desires become more defined and our passions more aroused. The Peace, Joy, Love, and Wisdom of the Soul drifts farther away. Then there is a desperate point in time in which we realize that self-empowerment, creation, co-creation, taking responsibility, visualizing, believing, affirming, and so on, just don't work. And we think there must be something wrong with us because it seems (operative word here—*seems*) to be working for everyone else. It is at this point that we yearn for the comfort and all embracing Love of the Divine Mother—we want to go Home. We are lonely, melancholy, and nothing seems to fit quite right. We are now ready for the Mystical Journey.

When we are truly ready (not just "sampling" another path), we will be guided along the way. Someone or something will show us a way to the very first step. We will be introduced to the True Teacher who is assigned by our Divine Mother to take us out of the ocean of suffering and dissatisfaction and back into Her Arms forever!

The mystical path is not always easy

but it is all there really is

when it is Everything that you want!

The Bigger, Bigger Picture

For a minute, let's let go of the small stuff and see it all from a bigger picture.

Let's "make believe" that just before creation occurred God brought all the Souls together, all those who were to go out through the various universes and planes to experience His creation for Him. Remember that the purpose of it all was for the Creator to experience the completeness of His Existence. He who is Unlimited has not experienced limitation and needs to have this experience in order to completely differentiate and be complete.

So, here we are, all gathered together and we are getting our assignments. And then God says, "I need some volunteers for the most difficult of all assignments. I need Souls to go to the earth plane to experience the worst of all possible conditions that I can imagine for Myself to experience. I will send you to a plane where you will become enchanted with the manifestations of light, sound, thought, and matter. It is a very dense plane. It is the densest in all of creation. It is also the one of greatest suffering, for you will forget your true nature, forget Me, and suffer greatly from the separation, loneliness, depression, disappointment, illness, and anxiety of trying to find Me and all of My gifts outside of yourself. You will have to endure many, many lifetimes. You will be deceived by false prophets and teachers who will promise you My Heaven on this earth. Your beautiful Soul nature will be covered with an ignorance— a state of ego consciousness, the false pseudo-soul. Worst of all, you will think I have forgotten you and don't love you. These conditions sadden Me greatly, but it is necessary that I achieve the nearly impossible on this earth plane, the most difficult and paradoxical of all experiences.

"I must fulfill the goal of my creation."

"I must experience My Unboundedness within boundaries. I must forget that I am One and think I am many. And when this has occurred, I must reverse the process of creation and find Myself again.

"Who loves me enough to accept this impossible and painful assignment? Who loves Me enough to endure and allow for My completion?"

And then a number of great hero Souls shouted out in unison "We, Lord! We, Lord. We love You and only You and we will show you the depth of our love by overcoming all obstacles that you place in our path. Send us!"

At that moment the human race was born
and God knew that He was loved beyond measure

And here we are, struggling and being human, trying to remember that we are God experiencing His creation through us.

From this perspective it is easier to be more compassionate with yourself and others...look around at the other hero Souls (no matter what state they are in) who have also volunteered to undergo the earth plane to fulfill the mission of creation. We are loved dearly by Love Itself...and when we reach our Home there will be joy and celebration without end!

Appendix A

The Bicycle Wheel:
Spiritual Progression

A very simple illustration of a bicycle wheel is sometimes very helpful in understanding the progression of creation and the spiritual journey back to the Source.

Consider the following blank page as the Absolute, Unbounded, Limitless God beyond all creation, the infinite potential to be in the unmanifest state of being.

At the first instant of creation, the Formless Unmanifest became the Mother God Creator. This is represented as a small circle in the center of the following page.

Although transcendent to all qualities, the nature of God is Existence (being), Consciousness (intelligent awareness), and Bliss (supreme Joy and self fulfillment).

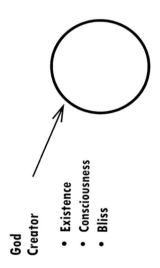

God
Creator
- Existence
- Consciousness
- Bliss

The large outer circle represents all of creation—all forms whether very subtle (etheric), energetic (astral), or gross (physical).

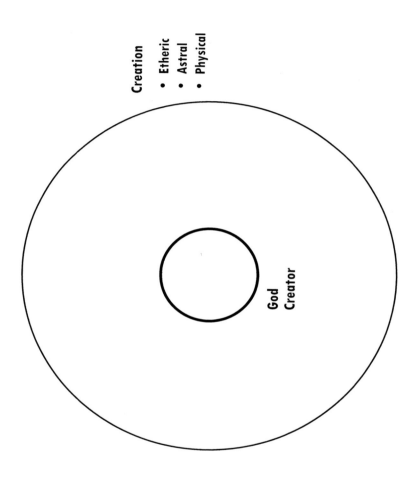

Creation
- Etheric
- Astral
- Physical

God
Creator

The Divine Mother-Creator aspect of God manifests individualized aspects of Herself known as "Souls." The purpose of these Souls is to experience Her creation. Each Soul manifests a personality—body, mind, and senses—to experience the etheric, astral, and physical elements of form or creation. The ego is not a thing per se, but a state of consciousness when the Soul mistakes its nature of being one with God as a separate nature comprised of the temporal personality and bound by birth/death.

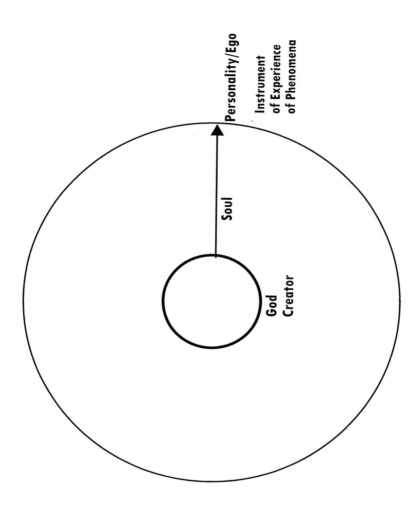

In the following illustration we see numerous "spokes"—all manner of creation—emanating from the Source, the inner circle, God the Creator. All attach to the larger circle with a "nub" similar to a real bicycle wheel. That "nub" is its own unique set of qualities or persona as well as the body, mind, and senses unit. Even particles on a sub-atomic level have characteristics of behavior given certain stimuli.

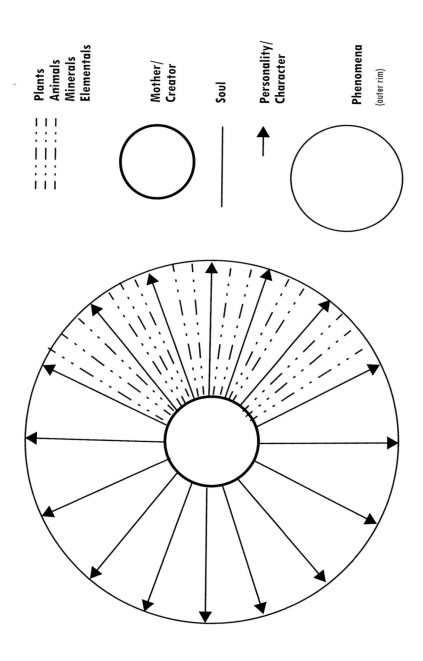

Plants
Animals
Minerals
Elementals

Mother/
Creator

Soul

Personality/
Character

Phenomena
(outer rim)

Now we can see clearly the progression of creation as a repulsion from Source—from God Unmanifest, Beyond Creation, through the Creator, to Soul to individual ego/personality.

The spiritual process is the reversal of the creation process wherein the individual consciousness expands from its contracted state to embrace its wholeness in the Essence of Unmanifest Limitless Source of Being.

Note: This is a very simple and primitive illustration. It is figuratively symbolic and not literally. It is a means to understand but it is not the understanding itself...a map but not the actual territory.

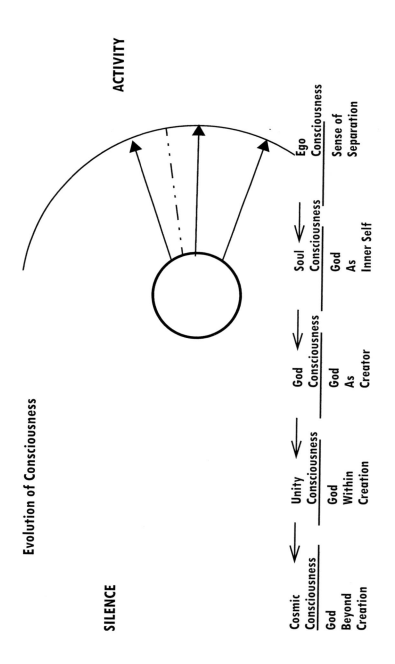

ACTIVITY

Evolution of Consciousness

SILENCE

Ego
Consciousness

Sense of
Separation

Soul
Consciousness

God
As
Inner Self

God
Consciousness

God
As
Creator

Unity
Consciousness

God
Within
Creation

Cosmic
Consciousness

God
Beyond
Creation

Appendix B

Resources

1. Anandamayi Ma, *As the Flower Sheds Its Fragrance*, Calcutta, India: Shree Shree Anandamayee Charitable Society (Available through the Blue Dove Foundation, www.bluedove.com, 858-623-3330)

2. Bacovin, Helen, translator, *The Way of a Pilgrim*, New York, NY: Doubleday Press

3. Burrows, Ruth, *Ascent to Love: the Spiritual Teachings of St. John of the Cross*, Denville, NJ: Dimension Books

4. Conway, Timothy, *Women of Power and Grace*, Santa Barbara, CA: Wake-Up Press

5. Dabholkal, Govind, translated by Nagest Vasudev Gunaji, *Shri Sai Satcharita, The Wonderful Life and Teachings of Shri Sai Baba*, Mumbai, India: Shri Sai Baba Sansthan. Call StillPoint Communications (603-434-2264) to order.

6. Keating, Thomas, *Invitation to Love*, Amity, NY: Amity House

7. Lawrence, Brother, translated by Robert J. Edmonson, *The Practice of the Presence of God*, Brewster, MA: Paraclete Press

8. Markides, Kyriacos, *The Mountain of Silence: A Search for Orthodox Spirituality*, New York, NY: Doubleday Press

9. Paramahansa Yogananda, *Autobiography of a Yogi*, Los Angeles, CA: Self-Realization Fellowship

10. Paramahansa Yogananda, *God Talks with Arjuna: The Bhagavad Gita*, Los Angeles, CA: Self-Realization Fellowship

11. Paramahansa Yogananda, *The Second Coming of Christ*, Dallas, TX: Amrita Foundation, Inc.

12. Prabhavananda, Swami, *The Sermon on the Mount According to Vedanta*, Hollywood, CA: Vedanta Society

13. Thomas, Jerry, *Heart of the Mystic: Contemplations of Mystical Wisdom*, Phoenix, AZ: Mystical Heart Press

14. Thomas, Jerry, *State of Grace,* Phoenix, AZ: Mystical Heart Press (available summer, 2003)

15. Thomas, Jerry, *Fullness of Life: Inner Silence,* Phoenix, AZ: Mystical Heart Press (available late 2003)

End Notes

1. Llewellyn Vaughan-Lee, *The Sufi Path of Love*.

2. T. S. Eliot

3. Matthew 5:48

4. Paramahansa Yogananda in *God Talks with Arjuna, the Bhagavad-Gita, the Royal Science of God-Realization*, Chapter 1, Verse 8.

5. Matthew 6:33, Luke 12.31

6. Matthew 16:26

7. Matthew 6:33

8. The illustration of the Bicycle Wheel in Appendix A illustrates the relationship between these states of consciousness.

9. Luke 12:31

10. Matthew 6:33

11. Ruth Burrows, *Ascent To Love*, Chapter 2.

12. *The Spiritual Canticle: Complete Works of John of the Cross*, Translated by Kavanaugh

13. ibid.

14. Ruth Burrows, *Ascent To Love*, Chapter 2.

15. ibid.

16. St. John of the Cross quoted in *Ascent To Love* by Ruth Burrows.

17. Serenity Prayer from Alcoholics Anonymous.

18. *Trustful Surrender To Divine Providence, The Secret of Peace and Happiness*, Fr. Jean Baptiste Saint-Jure, S.J., Blessed Claude De La Colombiere, S.J.

19. Matthew 6:10

20. Sufi saying, author unknown.

21. Charles Dickens, *The Tale of Two Cities.*

22. Paramahansa Yogananda, *Autobiography of a Yogi.*

23. Luke 12:31

24. This process, referred to as "Lexio Divina," is explained more fully in *Heart of the Mystic*, also by Jerry Thomas (due out in Spring, 2003).

25. Matthew 6:33

26. John 10:30

27. Matthew 10:39

28. Matthew 6:33

29. Matthew 22:37

30. This doesn't mean, for example, that we don't work hard to make the world a better place, but it does mean that after we have done whatever we can, we leave the results up to God and rest in the knowledge that everything is occurring according to Divine Will.

31. Sufi saying, author unknown.

32. John 8:32

33. This author is unknown, but I want to acknowledge the beautiful way in which he/she gave words to the Silence.

34. John 14:11

35. Matthew 5:48

36. Sufi saying, author unknown.

37. John 10:30

38. Matthew 22:37

39. John 15:12

40. A simple yet profound spiritual practice for those who aspire to God Realization is explained in depth in *Heart of the Mystic*, also by Jerry Thomas. It is scheduled to be released in Spring of 2003.

41. Sufi saying, author unknown.

42. Matthew 16:26

43. See *The Way of the Pilgrim* in the Resources section. Also see the section on Centering Prayer at www.greatpeace.net.

44. Anandamayi Ma, quoted in *Women of Power and Grace* by Timothy Conway.

45. Aisu Said as quoted by Pir Vilayt Kahn.

46. See note 24.

47. Amma Mata Amritanandamayi Ma, quoted in *Women of Power and Grace* by Timothy Conway.

48. These three qualities separate out mere teachers from those God-Realized Beings who can take you Home. No one short of one in complete union with God Himself can bestow these gifts upon a student.

49. Matthew 5:48

50. Matthew 5:48

51. Matthew 22:37

About the Author

Jerry Thomas is an accomplished philosopher, writer, teacher, lecturer, and practitioner of Mystical Spirituality. His broad and diverse education includes extensive study in modern sciences, comparative spirituality, mysticism, and world religions.

He has been a life-long participant and student of both Eastern and Western monastic traditions, with a formal education that includes advanced degrees in science, education, and organizational development.

He is currently the retreat master and founder of the StillPoint Retreats, which is a unique series of experiential seminars and workshops exploring Mystical Spirituality as a concept and an experience. In these silent retreat experiences, he teaches the principles of the mystical tradition as well as simple methods of attaining the fulfillment of the inner, Transcendent Self.

Jerry has two other books available that continue the themes covered in this book: *State of Grace* and *Heart of the Mystic*, both available through Mystical Heart Press.

You can contact Jerry Thomas through StillPoint Communications:

117 Walnut Hill Road
Derry, NH 03038, USA
(603) 434-2264
stillpoint@greatpeace.net
www.greatpeace.net

Seminars & Retreats

The StillPoint Silent Retreats, conducted by Jerry Thomas, are designed to provide a deep and abiding experience of the Inner Self, the essence and fulfillment of who we truly are. Each retreat is a balance of time-honored spiritual knowledge as taught by the Masters of the Mystical traditions of all world religions, as well as quiet periods of meditative silence. Simple practices are taught to allow the direct experience of the beautiful inner state from which all such spiritual knowledge flows. There are also periods of group and private meditation, contemplation, walks, rest, and individual study.

These retreats are for those who desire a deeper and more sustained relationship to their Inner Divinity as expressed in the experience of joy, wisdom, and profound inner peace. Although each weekend has a different theme, the core knowledge is that of the way of "Mystical Spirituality," with the focus on experiencing deep inner silence.

Retreats are kept small to maximize personal attention for each individual. No more than fifty participants are accepted for each event. These smaller groups are quieter and more focused.

For further information, contact:
StillPoint Retreats, Inc.
117 Walnut Hill Road
Derry, NH 03038, USA
(603) 434-6100
retreats@stillpointretreats.com
www.stillpointretreats.com